SLIM FINGERS BECKON

Other Books by ARCH MERRILL

SLIM FINGERS
BECKON

BY ARCH MERRILL

An enlarged and revised edition of
the Lakes Country, and including
Skaneateles, Owasco & Cayuga Lakes,
Not Covered in Previous Book

Some of the Material Appeared in the
Rochester N.Y. Democrat and Chronicle
in Serial Form

PRINTED IN THE UNITED STATES OF AMERICA
AMERICAN BOOK–STRATFORD PRESS, INC., NEW YORK

Contents

SLIM FINGERS BECKON

Chapter 1

Land of Lakes and Legends

There is an old Indian legend that the Finger Lakes came into being when the Great Spirit placed the imprint of his hand in blessing on the Upstate land.

Scientists will tell you that those long, slim streaks of blue in the center of the New York State map go back to the glacial age, that when the great ice sheet melted, its deposits dammed the parallel north and south valleys, which filled with water from springs and streams.

There are six major Finger Lakes. Reading from east to west, their names are Skaneateles, Owasco, Cayuga, Seneca, Keuka and Canandaigua. They are Indian names and sometimes strangers stumble a bit over their pronunciation.

West of the Big Six, in the uplands south of Rochester lie four "Little Finger Lakes." They are Honeoye, Canadice, Hemlock and Conesus. Carrying out the story of the blessing of the five-fingered god, it follows that he put all ten fingers on the land. Which also disposes of any dispute between Owasco and Keuka Lakes as to Finger Lake status.

This Lakes Country is singularly beautiful and singularly unsung. Some of its scenery is so spectacular the region has been called "The Switzerland of America." It is studded with waterfalls, especially in the southern edges. One of them is higher than Niagara Falls. Along many high-

1

ways, the motorist hears a sudden tinkle and he beholds a curtain of water splashing down from a hillside, almost into the roadway. A 140-foot cataract roars in the city of Ithaca. There are little waterfalls, never seen by tourists, in cottagers' backyards.

It is a land of magnificent gorges, romantic glens, eerie caverns and hills that a less conservative people would call mountains. It also has its pastoral side where the hills are gentle and the landscape is one of sylvan peace.

It is a mystical land of legends, this land of the Lake Guns, the Barren Hill, the Painted Rocks and the Burning Spring.

The spade of the archeologist has unearthed the bones of prehistoric settlers of at least 5,000 years ago. There are relics of a mound-building and other pre-Iroquois peoples.

The dawn of history saw the land divided among three Iroquois Nations of the Long House, the Onondagas, the Cayugas and the Senecas. Their names linger on our towns and counties, on our lakes and streams.

In 1779 when the fortunes of the rebellious colonies were at low ebb, George Washington sent an army under General John Sullivan of New Hampshire to invade the Indian country in the interior of York State. Sullivan's men cut a swath of desolation around the lakes. They destroyed scores of Indian villages and the encircling fields and orchards. Few Redskins ever returned to their old hunting grounds.

Sullivan was blazing a path of settlement as well as of ruin. For after the Revolution, many of his veterans, remembering the fairness of the land where long lakes shimmered in the Autumn sunshine, returned as settlers. Many of them

2

took lands on the Military Tract offered as bounty for their wartime services.

The region is sprinkled with classical names, such as Sempronius, Ithaca, Cato, Ovid, Lodi, Scipio, Romulus, Marcellus. It is said they were bestowed by some scholar in the state surveyor general's office who had to name the rapidly organizing new townships in a hurry after the Revolution.

Most of the frontier communities sprang up along the natural waterways. Often they rose on the site of the old Indian villages and generally the white man's highways followed the old Indian trails. There followed in procession the eras of the stage coach, the canal, the Iron Horse, the steamboats, electricity and gasoline.

Today in the old Indian land of lakes dwell more than a half million people. The boundaries of the Lakes Country are rather elastic, spreading over all or parts of eight counties. They include four cities, many flourishing villages and many drowsy hamlets. On the shores of the lakes are five colleges.

A great variety of crops are raised in the Lakes Country. Around Keuka and Canandaigua Lakes is one of the major grape and wine belts of the East. The region also has a bountiful yield of apples, peaches, cherries, pears and other fruits. Dairying is a considerable industry in the hills. Teasels and hops are among the Lakes Country's "ghost crops." Ithaca on Cayuga Lake and Watkins Glen on Seneca are centers of a considerable salt industry. Some of the salt is pumped from the lakes themselves.

The region has raised quite a crop of famous people— Logan and Red Jacket, the finest orators of the Six Nations;

3

one President, Millard Fillmore; William H. Seward, the Civil War statesman; an oil king, John D. Rockefeller, Sr., who lived as a boy around Owasco Lake; Jemima Wilkinson, the Universal Friend, founder of a strange religious colony; Marcus Whitman, the medical missionary of Oregon massacre fame; Bob Ingersoll, the silver-tongued "infidel," Glenn Curtiss, the pioneer of the airways, to name a few.

Her settlers were a mixture of Yankees, Pennsylvanians and Eastern York Staters, with a sprinkling of Southern gentry. On some rural mailboxes is the same name as that of the pioneer who first cleared that farm land. The Irish came to build the canals and the railroads and the Germans to raise grapes and other crops. At the turn of this century came the peoples of Southern and Eastern Europe to work in the Finger Lakes industries.

This land is the birthplace of the cast iron plow, the bloomer costume, and maybe, the ice cream sundae, among other things. It is the cradle of women's suffrage and of naval aviation.

Ithaca was a producing center of silent movies in the days of the serial thriller. The invention of an Auburn man led to the development of the sound movies.

For years the slim fingers have beckoned lovers of the beautiful. Some have come from far places. Watkins Glen has been a resort for 80 years. The advent of the horseless carriage and "hard roads" increased the popularity of the region for the tourists. Yet considering its natural beauty, its recreational facilities and its accessibility to the teeming cities of the East, New York State's lakes region is, to quote

4

one of its most famous residents, Samuel Hopkins Adams, the author, and sage of Owasco Lake, "an unsung Eden."

A representative of the State Department of Commerce last Summer addressing a meeting of the progressive Finger Lakes Association called the section, a "reluctant vacationland."

Maybe that is because of the innate conservatism of her people, their disinclination to "toot their own horn." Certainly it is not their lack of hospitality or willingness to share their beautiful land with others less fortunate.

Chapter 2

Skaneateles, the Eastern Gateway

During his long public career William Henry Seward made many pronouncements.

Some of them were considered highly important at the time. Few of them are remembered now. But one utterance of the statesman has never been allowed to die.

It was after a trip around the world that the man famous in history as Lincoln's secretary of state pronounced Skaneateles Lake "the most beautiful body of water in the world."

To this day the publicity of the Skaneateles Chamber of Commerce and other booster organizations repeat that quotation.

Seward's statement is particularly significant because he was a resident of Auburn, only seven miles away, and at the foot of another beautiful body of water, Owasco Lake. Few dwellers on any of the Finger Lakes have been given to superlative praise of a rival.

Skaneateles is the highest of the Finger Lakes, 867 feet above sea level. Hence it has been called "The Roof Garden" of the lakes. It is 15 miles long, one to two miles wide and in places 350 feet deep. Its spring-fed waters curve between hills that are gently rolling at its foot and that rise to majestic heights at its head. I have never seen it in an angry mood but I suppose it has its tantrums.

And I know of no more attractive community in Upstate New York than the distinctive and immaculate old village that bears the same name as the blue lake that borders its principal street, Genesee. Few village main streets have such a setting.

Skaneateles is an Indian name, translated as meaning "long lake." According to the best local authority, it is pronounced "Sken-ee-at-les," not as some tourists have it, "Skinny-atlas."

The 157-year-old village on the Cherry Valley Turnpike has an air of serenity yet it throbs with life. There are Summer days when the visitors outnumber the village population of around 2,000. And the cars parked along the lake front bear the license plates of virtually every state in the Union and some foreign countries.

Skaneateles is a stopping place for thousands of travelers, not only because of its scenic charm but also because it is known from coast to coast as the home of superb food—in generous servings. The name of Krebs has become synonymous with that of the village. Krebs is more than just an eating place. It has become an institution. There are other good places to eat in the lakeside village. I, for one, am happy that one of them, the Sherwood Inn, has resumed its old name. I never could pronounce Kan-ya-to correctly.

Syracuse, the Central New York metropolis, 18 miles to the northwest, should have a warm spot in its heart for the Finger Lake nearest its borders. For more than 50 years the city has drawn its pure water supply from the pretty lake in the hills. Many Syracusans have built Summer homes on its

7

shores and some of them have become year-around commuting residents. Through the years thousands of city folks have come down to the inland lake, if only for a day of recreation. In the old days they came by train or interurban trolley and the outing was not complete without a steamboat ride around the lake.

Now the steamboats are gone, along with the excursion trains and the interurbans. But still the Syracusans come to Skaneateles' cool and restful shores in the Summertime. But now they come by private auto or by motor bus.

Many Skaneateles residents work in Auburn and Syracuse. Little smoke of industry stains the neat homes of the village. The mills are to the north along the lake outlet at Mottville and Skaneateles Falls. Felt and chemicals are the principal products.

Although the village is in Onondaga County, of which Syracuse is the capital, it is close to the Cayuga County line and to the busy trading-manufacturing center of Auburn. Still nobody has ever dared to call Skaneateles a satellite of either city. The lakefront village stands on its own feet.

*   *   *

Skaneateles is in the old realm of the Iroquois Indian Confederacy. To the east were—and still are—the Onondagas. To the west were the Cayugas. The Indians felt the spell of the long blue lake and they fished in its waters and hunted on its wooded shores long before the white men came.

The first recorded visit of the palefaces was in 1750 when stout-hearted Moravian missionaries from Bethlehem, Pa.

built "the Pilgrim's Hut" of logs on St. John's Beach, near the present St. James Episcopal Church.

In 1779 a detachment of Sullivan's troops, 100 strong, bound for Albany after the colonial army had ravaged the Senecas' country, camped overnight at about the same spot.

Onondaga County was in the Military Tract, so called because its lands were offered as bounty to veterans of the Revolution in 1791. Three years later the first white settlers came to the site of Skaneateles. In the van was Abraham Cuddeback, who came through the woods from Orange County with his wife, eight children, a wagon, three yoke of oxen, a two-year-old colt and twelve cows. The journey over rough and narrow trails took 43 days.

In 1796 the Great Genesee Road, following the old central trail of the Indians, was opened from Utica to Canandaigua and down it passed many settlers. In 1800 the Seneca Turnpike, a wider, better road, built by private capital and paid for out of tolls, was begun. Generally it followed the Genesee Road.

At first the turnpike swung a mile and a half north of the present village but settlement gravitated toward the foot of the lake. The route was altered and there the village lots were laid out. Settlers bought some of them from Revolutionary veterans who got them as bounty. Also in 1800 the turnpike from Skaneateles to Cherry Valley, part of the present Route 20, was begun and Skaneateles, at the junction of two important highways, grew like the green bay tree.

The making of potash from the ashes of burned-off forests was an early industry. The potash was hauled by wagon to Albany and bartered for merchandise. In 1797 a log dam was built at the foot of the lake to provide added water power for the mills that sprang up along the Outlet. It raised the level of the lake four feet. Previously there had been a ford at its foot and a man could walk with his head above water on a sand bar from Shotwell Point to Mile Point.

In the early days carriages and sleighs made in the village were noted for the fancy designs painted upon them. For there were craftsmen, as well as farmers, among the pioneers. There also were a few aristocrats, who kept slaves, built mansions and wore the knee breeches, tricorn hats and buckled shoes of the gentry.

One notes a New England influence in the architecture of the older houses. That is because there lived in the village from 1812 to 1820 an artisan who came directly from Salem, Mass. It was he who built the "Salem doorways" and added other touches that make the old homes of Skaneateles so distinctive.

On the pioneer scene Isaac Sherwood, the stage coach king, cast a giant shadow, for he weighed nearly 300 pounds. At first he carried the mails on foot, then on horseback. In 1809 he and a partner formed a stage coach company, the Old Mail Line, that snared the contract for carrying the mails between Utica and Canandaigua.

By 1815 there were 15 stages rumbling daily into Skaneateles and stopping at the original Sherwood Inn, which the stage coach magnate had built around 1800. His line had agents in all the principal places served by its stages and in one year it received $60,000 for carrying the mails, to say nothing of the passenger revenues.

The Sherwood coaches had all the stage business along the

central turnpike until 1828 when the Pioneer Line was formed to challenge the monopoly. The new line got control of the only large hotel in Auburn for its headquarters and refused accommodations to the horses and patrons of the Old Mail Line. Sherwood struck back by establishing his headquarters in another, newly-built Auburn hotel and by installing, under a new name, the Telegraph Line, a fleet of new light coaches, carrying only six passengers each and built for speed. He won the war. The Pioneer Line failed to get the mail contract and quit the field.

Isaac's son, John M. Sherwood, was almost as big and just as resourceful as his father. After the pioneer Syracuse and Auburn Railroad had been completed in the 1830s, all but laying the iron rails, John Sherwood obtained a short-term lease of the road, placed wooden rails on the string pieces and operated the line by horse power until the company could procure its rails. The whistle of the Iron Horse silenced the thunder of the stage coaches within a few years.

The Syracuse and Auburn Railroad bypassed Skaneateles, five miles to the north. So in 1836 local capital built a wooden railroad to connect with the Auburn Road at Skaneateles Junction. Horses drew its single coach. After 14 years it was succeeded by a plank road. In 1867 a steam railroad was constructed over the route. One of the shortest railroads in the land and locally owned, it is still in operation. Passenger service was abandoned some years ago but in its time the short line hauled many a trainload of Syracuse excursionists, bound for the lake and its steamboat rides.

Once the president of the little Skaneateles railroad was attending a meeting in New York, along with executives of some of the nation's biggest roads. Ways of keeping traffic moving in snow storms came up and the Skaneateles man observed it was a big problem for his road.

Politely the head of a great trunk system asked:

"How long is your road?"

"Five miles," was the reply.

"Hell, build a roof over it," snorted the big operator.

* * *

Some famous names, and a few infamous ones, have been linked with the history of the village.

Old histories mention that in the early days of the 19th century Henry Arnold, a brother of Benedict, the traitor, lived three years in Skaneateles.

More space is given to Amos Miner. He came to the village in 1800 and he was an inventive genius. While on a sick bed, he thought up a spinning wheel head which saved pioneer women much hand and foot work. He devised a pail-making machine and a saw which gave its staves cylindrical form. He also invented a machine for making window sash. A United States Superintendent of Patents once observed: "Amos Miner of Skaneateles N. Y. in his time invented more useful machines than any other man in the country."

From 1843 to 1845 the region was the scene of an experiment in communism. On a 300-acre farm two miles north of the village a little group of Utopians, led by a John Anderson Collins, established a colony and advertised for followers. The group was dedicated to the holding of property in common, negation of all force, easy divorce and vegetarianism. The colony was a flop. There were too many free

12

boarders, too much internal friction and too much outside criticism.

More distinguished early residents were Dr. William M. Beauchamp, onetime state archeologist whose researches shed new light on Indian customs and places of habitation, and Leonard Jerome, who in his youth clerked in a Skaneateles store and read law in the village. He became a publisher in Rochester and later a prominent figure in commerce and society in New York City but is best known to fame as the grandfather of Winston Churchill.

Another illustrious name linked to Skaneateles is that of Roosevelt. Nicholas Roosevelt, a member of the New York clan with as many branches as a willow tree, lived in the village from 1831 to 1854. He was an inventor, interested in sailing and steamboats. The old Roosevelt place stands in Genesee Street.

In 1899 S. Montgomery Roosevelt purchased the white pillared mansion at the foot of the lake that was renamed Roosevelt Hall. It was the Summer residence of the late Henry Latrobe Roosevelt, who served as assistant secretary of the navy under his kinsman, FDR. Roosevelt Hall was the scene of a brilliant society wedding that united a daughter of the Democratic Roosevelts with a son of the Republican house of Wadsworth in the Genesee Valley. Roosevelt Hall now is owned by William Delevan.

In the grim early days of World War 2 when the Japanese were winning the Battle of the Pacific, a woman came back to the village of her girlhood where she had been Adele Holley. She lived in a West Genesee Street apartment with her mother, Mrs. Dwight Holley, for three tense years.

13

Her husband was a professional soldier. He was away fighting in the Philippines. The name of Jonathan Mayhew Wainwright will forever be associated with the heroic American defense of Bataan and Corregidor against overwhelming odds. His wife called the general "Skinny." To him she was "Kitty."

Corregidor finally fell and General Wainwright was made a prisoner of the Japanese. To the anxious woman in Skaneateles whose hair was graying came an occasional censored letter from a prison camp. The Japanese sent out a propaganda broadcast that the general was "well and comfortably housed." In July, 1943 Mrs. Wainwright went on the air in a dramatic broadcast to her husband. "Everything at home is fine," she said. "I am an airplane spotter. Johnny (their son, then 30, and in the Merchant Marine) has his own ship now. . . . Remember my love is always with you and keep faith until we are together again. Good night, Skinny, and God bless you." Thousands heard the brave words but they never reached her "Skinny" in his prison.

The long vigil ended on August 19, 1945 when, after the Japanese surrender, word came to Adele Wainwright in Skaneateles that her husband had been liberated. On September 10 "Skinny" and his "Kitty" were "together again." After four years they were reunited before cheering thousands at a sun-splashed Washington airport where the general had stepped from a plane. There was a big parade, speeches and a Congressional Medal of Honor for the hero of Corregidor, tired, white and thinner than ever.

Then the Wainwrights "came home" to Skaneateles. The general had never lived there but he had been a frequent visitor and as Mayor Jerome Murphy declared in his proclamation of a civic holiday, the military hero was "the husband of a Skaneateles lady who has made her home among us during the war."

The Finger Lakes village went all out with a parade and a dinner at which Robert P. Patterson, then secretary of war, spoke. The villagers still talk about it and a large picture of General Wainwright, Skaneateles' adopted son, hangs in the dining room of the Sherwood Inn for the tourists to see.

* * *

White sails on blue water—that picture has been linked with Skaneateles for considerably over a century.

The delayed launching of the first sail boat on the lake occurred in 1816. In 1812 a village grandee, Col. William J. Vredenbergh, drove his carriage all the way to his former home in New York to bring back a competent builder for his boat. The colonel died the next year before it was completed. Others finished the job and what had been intended as a private pleasure craft was launched under the name of the Four Sisters in 1816, the first of many excursion boats on the lake.

The first regattas were held in the 1840s. Boats were hauled over land from Cayuga and Seneca Lakes and the cream of the inland skippers competed for the silver plate and other prizes donated by Nicholas Roosevelt and fellow enthusiasts. In 1854 the first yacht club was formed. It was called the Skaneateles Model Yacht Club and the word, model, denoted excellence and not miniature boats.

The Civil War halted that glamorous era but the sport was revived in the later years of the century and since then the lake has been the scene of some major sailing events, including one international and two national regattas. The 1948 Central New York regatta, which attracted 169 craft of various classes, was hailed—locally at least—as the largest inland sailing event ever.

Many a steamboat has churned the waters of the lake. The first was the Independent, 80 feet long and the village, which had financed its construction, launched it with fitting ceremony on July 4, 1831. A license to operate it had to be obtained from Robert Fulton because the inventor at that time had a steamboat monopoly in the state. The Independent soon had a rival in the 40-foot Highland Chief which came up from New York via the Hudson and the Erie Canal and overland haul the rest of the way.

Other excursion boats were the Homer and the Skaneatales, both launched in the late 1840s; the Ben H. Porter, named after a Civil War hero, a round bottomed, rather unseaworthy craft which in 1873 capsized at its landing because of the weight of snow on its deck.

Then came the 180-foot Glen Haven, the Ossahinta and the last and best remembered, because of its moonlight excursions, the City of Syracuse, which, after a year spent in its construction, began operations in 1899. It carried 500 passengers and it was the finest steamboat ever to sail the lake. When it docked for the last time in 1914, the curtain fell on 83 picturesque years of steamboating on Skaneateles Lake.

There are hundreds of modest Summer homes around the lake's 30 miles of curving shoreline, as well as some palatial

16

ones around its foot. They are occupied by people from near and far. A Summer vacation on "the most beautiful body of water in the world" is something to look forward to.

Nestling among the hills and the farmlands on the lake or near its shores are several villages. They bear such foreign-sounding names as Sempronius, Borodino and Mandana, which are offset by such pioneer American names as Scott and Spafford. One bears the optimistic name of New Hope.

At Spafford, east of the lake, Joseph Smith, the Mormon prophet, recruited many converts and some of them who went West with the Saints rose to high places in the church. In the district school at Scott, south of the lake, years ago a blond young teacher, a native of the Moravia region and with little education himself, put down by force a revolt of the bigger boys. His name was Millard Fillmore.

Near New Hope, a half mile west of the lake, is one of those picturesque waterfalls you run across almost anywhere in the Lakes Country. It is Carpenter's Falls where a slender sheet of water cascades over a 100-foot cliff. Once those falls powered several mills.

At Glen Haven at the head of the lake, there was established in 1841 one of America's pioneer water cures. Its operator, Dr. W. C. Thomas, proved to the world the health-giving properties of his spa by living to the age of 107 years. Before Glen Haven had its own postoffice, it issued its own postage and claimed to be the only place in the state to do so. Now the only vestiges of the water cure are the words, Glen Haven, spelled out by white stones on a cottage lawn.

There are many venerable homes in the village of Skaneateles which reflect the good taste of their builders.

Probably the oldest is the charming white residence of Rod Benton on West Genesee Street, adjoining his book and antique shop. It goes back to 1798.

Memories of pre-Civil War days when Skaneateles was a station on the Underground Railway haunt 136-year-old Evergreen House on East Genesee Street. The white colonial style house, whose green blinds match its evergreen grove, once housed many a fugitive Negro, bound for Canada and freedom. According to tradition, Lafayette was a guest there when he made his grand tour of the region in 1825. An aide of the French Marquis recorded in his journal that when the party reached the village, candles in every window beamed a welcome. The services of "Mr. Sherwood, proprietor of the stage coaches," also are acknowledged.

Skaneateles has an art gallery, a rather unusual one. Built around the smaller gray brick structure that was Benoni Lee's law office and which after his death became the village library is the "annex" housing the Barrow Memorial Art Gallery, the gift in 1888 of John Barrow who was a poet as well as a painter. Many of the paintings are of regional scenes. Most of them came from the brush of John Barrow.

The pretty park at the foot of the lake which adds to the attractiveness of the business section was the gift of Mrs. William J. Shotwell and bears her name.

Nearby is a white frame building with a generous lawn. It is not a pretentious structure but it is the one that has given Skaneateles its widest fame. There in 1899 a native son, Fred R. Krebs, opened a small eating place with the idea of providing his patrons with all they could eat of the best possible food. It was a sound idea and the renown of Krebs spread, especially after the advent of the automobile and paved roads. The little inn had to be enlarged. By 1915 people either had to make reservations for their meals or wait in line, sometimes for as long as two hours. By 1920 Krebs was serving 3,000 meals on Summer Saturdays and Sundays, besides operating to capacity the rest of the week. Fred Krebs is dead but his adopted son, Frederick Perkins, carries on in the Krebs tradition. Today if you want to eat at Krebs and don't care to stand in line, you'd better make a reservation.

When the name, Skaneateles, is mentioned, most people immediately mention Krebs and the other excellent eating places in the village. And then they will invariably add: "Oh, yes, that's the village where they don't have to pay any taxes."

But mention that tax-free status to a resident, especially one of the older ones, and the atmosphere takes on a sudden chill. You are likely to hear the word, "phony." It is true, they will tell you, that for three years in the 1930s, the village levied no taxes.

They will explain that the freedom from taxes was achieved by the device of putting the rates of the municipally owned water and power services so high that no taxes were necessary. It was sort of "robbing Peter to pay Paul" but Skaneateles received wide publicity as a taxless community. Then the State Public Service Commission stepped in and ordered the rates reduced. Since then, the villagers have paid taxes although the rate, currently $12.073 per $1,000, is relatively low.

Skaneateles has another and a more genuine claim to fame. For more than a century virtually all the teasels cultivated in America came from the fields of Skaneatales and Marcellus townships in Onondaga County.

No doubt you have seen the teasel growing wild along the roads. A member of the thistle family, it bears a large bur or flower bud covered with stiff, prickly awns. No one has ever called it "the most beautiful plant in the world." The wild teasels are without commercial value but not so with the cultivated ones.

The teasel when cured provides the best known method of raising the nap on woolen cloth. The hooked awns on the extremities of the bur spines draw the fine fiber or hairs of the wool from the woven cloth, leaving a fine surface finish. Its use goes back to the days of the Roman Empire.

Around 1840, an English emigrant, familiar with the use of the teasel in woolen mills of his homeland, brought the first seeds to Skaneateles. The soil of the region was found ideal for cultivation of the plant. Two growing years are required before the teasel is ready for harvesting, which usually is in August.

Once hundreds of men and women gathered the crop in the hills around Skaneateles. They wore mittens or gloves to protect their hands against the nettles and after cutting the teasels from their stalks, carried them in large baskets to the barns where they were cured. In the Winter they were trimmed to the proper size, with a stick resembling the one on a lollipop.

Teasel merchants bought them by the pound. The industry flourished for 90 years. The biggest buyers in the region were the McLaughlin brothers, James and Cornelius, natives of England and early birds in the business. J. Ray McLaughlin, son of Cornelius and present village clerk of Skaneatales, carried on the business after the brothers passed on. He recalled that the biggest years in his time were 1924 and 1925 when he paid as high as 50 cents a pound for teasels. Around 1930 the bottom fell out of the market. Introduction of machinery to supplant the teasel and increased imports from France were contributing factors.

Now the teasel is almost a ghost crop. Two of the McLaughlin clan, John and Frank, cousins of J. Ray, carry on the family tradition. They grow some teasels themselves and buy some from farmers. But it's nothing like the old days when Skaneateles was "Teaseltown" and its fields produced virtually the entire crop cultivated in America.

*   *   *

Before we leave Skaneateles, a parting tip to tourists:

If your fancy runs to night life, strip teasers, Coney Islandish hubbub, glitter, garishness and a wild and woolly time, you won't care much for Skaneateles, N. Y.

But if you respond to the serene charm of a tidy, homelike village, facing a long blue lake, set in a frame of emerald hills; if you enjoy eating good food—and plenty of it—in such surroundings and among well-behaved people, Skaneateles, the old stage coach town on the Cherry Valley Turnpike, beside "the most beautiful body of water in the world," is just what you are looking for.

Chapter 3

Owasco

AND AUBURN, LAKES COUNTRY METROPOLIS

Owasco Lake is a sapphire gem of purest ray serene seemingly born to shimmer unseen, away from the casual tourist's gaze.

That's because the Indians and the copy-cat white pioneers built their towns and made their trails two and one half miles north of the foot of the hill-girt lake.

So today the tourist, inching his way through the traffic of Auburn, an industrial city of 36,000 at the junction of Upstate's two major highways, Routes 5 and 20, does not see the calm blue radiance of the lake that bears the old Indian name of Owasco, which means "the crossing."

But the home folks know and love Owasco. It is their lake, little spoiled by outlander invasion. There they find peace and beauty at the close of shop or office day. Most of the Summer homes, "camps" they call them, are lived in all Summer, not just a couple of weeks. The lake is the home folks' playground, "swimming hole," happy hunting and fishing ground, sailing course. For oldsters Owasco holds fond memories of excursion days and the great sculling and sailing races of yesteryear. And it was the swift water of the river-outlet which powered the pioneers' mills and gave Auburn being. It also gives the city its pure water supply.

Owasco is the smallest of the Finger Lakes but it is no puddle. It is 12 miles long and is 177 feet deep at one point. Its greatest width is one and one half miles. It is 720 feet above sea level. Its waters curve between two ridges in the familiar Lakes Country pattern.

Waterfalls, that few strangers see, tinkle in its glens. The highways that border the lake do not lead to large places and they are not overcrowded. Owasco is a peaceful, homey sort of lake.

Around its rugged head stretches the farm countryside where a President of the United States, Millard Fillmore, was born and where an oil king, John D. Rockefeller, lived as a boy.

At its foot smoke the chimneys of Auburn on its many hills, peopled by those of many bloods. Auburn is the largest city in the land of the slim blue lakes.

It has been a manufacturing and trading center since pioneer days. It is the shire town of Cayuga County and the cultural and political hub of its region. Once it aspired to become the capital of the state and its Capitol Street is an echo of that long faded dream.

It is a city of many facets. Those of foreign extraction form a large and interesting segment of its population. They are inclined to have their own colonies, clubs and churches. The Poles, Italians and Ukranians are the most numerous.

It has its wide and shady avenues, like South Street, lined with dignified public buildings and residences, many of them Victorian, in which "the upper crust" has lived for generations. Most of those mansions were built from the fortunes made from harvesters, cordage, shoes and other Auburn industries.

Auburn, named after Goldsmith's "loveliest village of the plain," is a city of distinguished history. Men and women famous in their time have called Auburn home—William H. Seward, the statesman, Harriet Tubman, the Negro "Joan of Arc," Thomas Mott Osborne, the crusader for prison reform, Logan, the Indian orator, to name a few.

But to many people—far too many, its boosters feel—Auburn is "the Prison City," the home of New York State's first prison. The metal figure of Copper John, the musket-bearing Revolutionary soldier, who for 128 years has stood guard over the gray walls of the prison, casts a massive shadow. The history of Auburn Prison is a grim one, at times a bloody one, but the pages are brightened by the stirring story of penological reform, written slowly and painfully through the years.

This city at the crossroads of the Empire State, has a diverting personality but I fear the average motorist on Routes 5 and 20 is too intent on his traffic chores to catch it. And one of our loveliest inland lakes is two and one half miles from the crossroads—and he doesn't see it.

*   *   *

Auburn's first settlers came before the dawn of recorded history. A few years ago excavations for a trolley loop at the foot of Owasco Lake turned up some Algonkian pottery with an estimated age of 800 years.

Fort Hill, now a cemetery, reputedly was the site of an ancient Indian fortress. The modern village of the Cayugas,

White Sails on Blue Skaneateles Waters

William H. Seward Mansion at Auburn

Wasco, was at State and Wall Streets, in the heart of the present city. Wasco added an "O" to its handle somewhere along the line. The Cayuga village was at the junction of two trails, just as the white man's city is today.

It was at Wasco, according to tradition, that Logan (Tah-gah-jute) who is ranked with the Seneca, Red Jacket, as the peer of Indian orators, was born around 1727. Red Jacket came later and he was an imitator of Logan.

Logan was born to the tribal purple. He inherited chieftainship over Pennsylvania tribes. He was a sachem of the Shamokins and of the Cayugas. Because of his silver tongue he often was chosen to represent the Six Nations at powwows with the whites.

In 1779 he moved down the Ohio River to Yellow Creek. There an English leader of a band of ruffians who specialized in massacre of Indians killed every member of Logan's family. The chief went on the warpath and 30 white scalps dangled from his belt. Shortly thereafter Logan made his greatest speech, at a conference with the British governor of Virginia. His words have been put into school textbooks as a model of eloquence:

"There runs not a drop of my blood in the veins of any living creature. This has called upon me for revenge. I have sought it. I have killed many. I have fully glutted my vengeance. For my country I rejoice at the beam of peace. But do not harbor the thought that mine is the joy of fear. Logan never felt fear. He will never turn on his heel to save his life. Who is there to mourn for Logan? Not one."

Like Red Jacket, Logan became intemperate in his later years. While under the influence of firewater, he was killed by a kinsman along the Ohio in 1781. His bones were brought back to Fort Hill, near his birthplace.

In 1852 through funds raised by popular subscription, the citizens of Auburn raised an obelisk of the native limestone to the orator of the tribes. It towers 56 feet above his grave and dominates the hillside cemetery where sleep the elite of Auburn, the Sewards, the Osbornes, the Cases, the Willards and the rest. On it is a simple inscription: "Who is there to mourn for Logan?"

Two years before Logan died, a party of Sullivan's troopers passed through the site of Auburn on their eastward march to Albany. Their leader was Col. Peter Gansevoort. After the Revolution, like many another veteran, he returned —as a settler.

Another officer of Sullivan's command was the father of Auburn. He was Capt. John L. Hardenbergh, a tall, swarthy Dutchman, who had been awarded Military Tract land in Fabius but chose instead a site beside the Owasco outlet in the then Town of Aurelius. In 1793 he came to stay, with a daughter and two Negro slaves. He built a log cabin in the rear of the present City Hall and then a grist mill.

Other settlers came down the Genesee Road and a settlement sprang up, called Hardenbergh's Corners. Soon there were several mills along the Owasco and a tavern where the stage coaches stopped.

By 1803 its citizens felt the need of a more dignified name for their growing community than Hardenbergh's Corners. Some were for shortening the name to Hardenbergh. Others favored Mount Maria. But the majority of "the naming committee" voted for Auburn, after "the loveliest village of the plain" in the Goldsmith poem. Some of the minority sniffed at the connotation of a "deserted village."

But Auburn did not languish into any deserted village. It became the fastest growing place in the region, rivaling the older villages of Canandaigua and Geneva. By 1808 it had its first newspaper. By 1809 it boasted 250 people. That was the year it captured the county seat from Aurora on Cayuga Lake.

In 1810, with the canal bee buzzing in his head, De Witt Clinton visited Auburn on a tour of the state and wrote in his journal of 14 mills along the Owasco Outlet, including one that made linseed oil from flaxseed broken by two mill stones. He also noted that oil was made from the seed of sunflowers.

When finally Clinton's Ditch was dug across the state in 1825, it swung north of Auburn through more level country. It was a blow but the "loveliest village" on its many hills found solace in its new state prison and its new Presbyterian theological seminary.

*　　*　　*

Copper John has stood guard over the gray-walled city within a city for 128 years but the prison is older than he.

Auburn worked hard to capture the state prison site and her citizens donated the land beside the Owasco on which it was built. Construction began on June 28, 1816, with the laying of the southwest cornerstone of the 20-foot high wall. A bottle of whiskey was placed in it. Presumably it is still there.

The prison received its first inmates in 1817 although the

main building was not completed until 1820 and the entire wall not until 1823. That was the year Copper John mounted to his pinnacle. The metal figure was made by an Auburn craftsman. He has become a landmark of his city, but, its citizens hope, never its symbol. No one inside the prison walls has ever seen the old soldier face to face. He looks out on the street—and the free world. He has seen so much in his long vigil. He has watched the gates clang shut behind many a man and many a woman who never went out.

In 1821 before the prison was completed, reformers pushed through a law providing for solitary cells as an improvement over herding of prisoners. But the law did not specify the size of the cells and economy-minded officials made them the smallest area in which a man could both lie down and sit up, 3½ feet by 7 by 7. These cages were built in rows, back to back, and several tiers high. They formed America's first cell block and provided the pattern for prison construction for a hundred years.

From the beginning, hiring out of convict labor on contracts was found to be profitable for all concerned, except the prisoners. In 1823 the "silent system" was instituted. Prisoners were marched lockstep to the contract shops and fields where they worked from sunup to sunset, all in strict silence. Guards carried whips to enforce the rule.

Auburn convicts built Sing Sing Prison in 1825. They helped construct the Erie Canal Aqueduct at Rochester. From 1837 to 1842 in the prison shops they made silk cloth from cocoons produced by silkworms in mulberry trees, brought in from growers of the region. The inclement New York State climate made that industry a short-lived one. Incidentally, Auburn prisoners have been making state auto license plates since 1920.

The shower bath punishment was devised at Auburn Prison in 1849, replacing the lash. The offender was fastened in the stocks and ice-cold water poured over him. In 1859 the first asylum for the criminal insane in the world was established at Auburn. It became the women's prison in 1893 when Matteawan was opened for the state's insane criminals.

It was at Auburn in 1890 that a Buffalo murderer, William Kemmler, was put to death in the first electric chair in the world. That chair (or at least the sign on it said so) for years was a prize item in the strange collection of curios that Rattlesnake Pete Gruber housed in his celebrated museum-saloon in Rochester. Before executions were shifted to Sing Sing in 1916, 57 had been electrocuted at Auburn, among them Leon Czolgosz, the assassin of President McKinley, and Chester Gillette of "American Tragedy" fame.

Prison reform has been a long, slow process. Gone are the yoke, the ball and chain, the lash, compulsory silence, the striped suit, contract labor and other things that seem almost medieval today. But they lasted a long time. Contract labor was not abolished until 1882. Compulsory silence and the lockstep lingered until 1898.

In 1913 a new and glittering chapter in prison reform began. The author was a rich, young, idealistic Auburnian, Thomas Mott Osborne, son of the founder of an important harvester industry. Tom Osborne became interested in penological methods through his work with the George Junior Republic at Freeville where William "Daddy" George was experimenting with self government as a cure for juvenile delinquency.

Named state prison commissioner in 1913, Osborne began his duties by serving a week behind Auburn's walls under the name of Tom Brown. He wrote a book, "Behind Prison Walls," that drew national attention to prison conditions. He founded in Auburn Prison a Mutual Welfare League under which the convicts had a form of self government and discipline.

His league ended in a welter of blood and the rattle of gunfire in 1929, a year Auburn will never forget. It was the year of two gory prison riots.

The first one shattered the calm of Sunday afternoon, July 28, when rioters seized the arsenal and fired several prison buildings. Before the battle was over six hours later, two convicts were dead, one prisoner, three guards and a state trooper lay wounded, four convicts had escaped over the wall (they were captured later) and a $500,000 fire had ruined eight buildings.

The riot leaders were severely punished but an ugly spirit of unrest smoldered in the prison. It erupted into the bloodiest prison riot in New York State history on December 11, when a little band of desperate men, some of them lifers, seized the warden, Gen. Edgar S. Jennings, and several guards. Holding them as hostages, they overpowered other guards, seized guns and for a time controlled the prison. State troopers, National Guardsmen and police from Auburn, Rochester, Syracuse and Geneva were rushed in. There was a fierce battle in which tear gas played a conquering role and Warden Jennings was rescued. At twilight it was all over but eight convicts and the principal keeper were dead and eight other men were wounded. Not a prisoner escaped.

The second riot brought an investigation which resulted in reconstruction of outmoded, century-old buildings, building of some new walls and general modernization of the plant at a cost of four million dollars. General Jennings, who had commanded a regiment in the first World War, was relieved of his prison command.

Since then a general calm has reigned at the prison. The model new state prison at Attica in the Wyoming County hills has taken much of the load off Auburn. Now no prisoners are sent directly to Auburn. Its 1,612 inmates are transfers from other prisons.

But Copper John still casts his shadow over the metropolis of the Finger Lakes. Armed guards still pace the new walls between the sentry boxes as they did the old. Once in a while Auburnians hear the wail of the siren that tells of an escape and see the glare of the floodlights.

But much as Auburn people dislike the emphasis put on its status as a prison city, they can't ignore its payroll of some 500 employees. The old prison must be classed as a considerable Auburn industry, despite its grim overtones.

*   *   *

While the walls of the prison were still rising, in May 1820 on a distant hill the cornerstone was laid for the Auburn Theological Seminary of the Presbyterian denomination. Convicts helped break the ground and the seminary admitted its first students on Oct. 15, 1821. The growing town

31

of 2,200 was proud of its two new institutions, the prison and the divinity school.

The prison is still there but the seminary is no more. There are those who wish the reverse were true. After 118 years of training ministers, the school closed its doors in May of 1939. A movement for a merger with the Baptist Colgate-Rochester Divinity School in Rochester failed and it became a part of Union Theological Seminary in New York City.

In 1946 part of the plant, on its 17-acre campus which covers four city blocks, was taken over for veterans' housing. The 1951 visitor to the campus finds GIs and their families living in the five-story Morgan Hall dormitory and Negro families occupying Welch Memorial Hall. Morgan Library is boarded up and so is Willard Memorial Chapel.

In the rear of the old chapel the washing of GI families flap from clotheslines. Children, black and white, play on the swings and slides under the old campus trees. And the days when earnest young divinity students walked to classes across that campus seem far away indeed.

*   *   *

When Lafayette visited Auburn in 1825, he was greeted by band music, an arch of boughs, flowers and a speech by a young lawyer. William Henry Seward was his name and although he had lived in the village only two years he was a coming man. He was a slender, beardless, red-haired, blue-eyed, eagle-beaked young man with genial manners, a platform presence, and an eternal cigar.

He had come from his native Orange County in 1823 at the age of 21 to practice law in the office of Judge Elijah

Miller, a leading man of the town. Seward was an ambitious fellow who mixed politics with the law. He started his climb in time-honored fashion by marrying the boss's daughter. The Sewards lived in the big gray brick house at 33 South Street which the judge had built in 1816. After the judge died, it became "the Seward Mansion."

Seward was on the threshold of his political career when in 1824 his coach broke down in Rochester and a burly young editor of that mill town, Thurlow Weed, came to his aid. There began a lasting personal friendship and a political alliance that made history. Weed moved to Albany and became Whig boss of the state. His fondest dream was of making his friend, Bill Seward, President of the United States. He had much to do with the Auburnian's nomination and election to the governorship in 1838 and his later elevation to the United States Senate.

They made an effective team. Weed, shrewd, bluff, realistic, with little formal education but a keen knowledge of men, was the behind-the-scenes manipulator, the master of the lobby, the caucus, the committee room. Seward, affable, glib, of cultivated manners yet studiously careless in his dress, an opportunist with a flair for oratory and the apt phrase, sometimes a dreamer, was the "front man." He went out among the voters.

The Auburn politico rose to national prominence as the spokesman of the anti-slavery forces of the North. Seward was no puppet of Weed. They worked together and between the two there was a real affection but Seward was his own man and made his own decisions. His daring reference during a Senate debate on the free soil issue to a "higher Law than the Constitution" and his prophecy in a Rochester address of "an irrepressible conflict" were widely quoted.

In 1856 when the new Republican party entered the arena, Seward was its outstanding figure. He held back from the Presidential race that year, sensing defeat. He and his mentor were waiting for 1860. When the Republican convention met in the Wigwam at Chicago in May of that year, there was every indication that its choice would be William H. Seward.

Weed commanded the Seward forces in Chicago. Seward stayed in the mansion in Auburn. His Auburn neighbors hauled a cannon on the Seward lawn, ready to fire it the instant word was flashed from Chicago of their fellow townsman's nomination.

Alas, they had to haul their cannon home, unfired. A little known Illinois politician, Abraham Lincoln, had won the prize. His managers had made some deals, vengeful Horace Greeley had gotten even with his onetime partners, Weed and Seward, and for once the New York boss had been outmaneuvered. Weed wept openly in the Convention. His friend, Bill Seward, would never be President.

But he did become Lincoln's Secretary of State and went down in the history books as one of the foremost statesman of a critical time. His purchase of Alaska from the Russians at two cents an acre was derided at the time as "Seward's Folly" but time has vindicated Seward's judgment.

He was gravely wounded in the plot that assassinated Lincoln but stuck to his post until a new order, not to his taste, moved in with General Grant. Seward was fastidious, for a politician. He died in the mansion in 1872.

Until this year his descendants have lived in the big house, where the stone lions crouch at the gateway pillars and griffins guard the stately entrance, the mansion with the spacious grounds, the many chimneys and fan windows where royalty and political potentates have wined and dined. The last of the line, William H. Seward 3d, a grandson of the statesman, died a few months ago. The house is to be preserved under a foundation as a historic landmark, housing much of Seward's furniture and other effects. His papers recently were presented to the University of Rochester Library, where students of history may read them along with those of his old partner, Thurlow Weed.

Near the mansion in a little park the statesman stands in bronze and a famous name lives in the lettering on a window of the 90-year-old private banking house of William H. Seward & Company in downtown Auburn.

Seward was not the first Auburn man to be New York's governor. From 1829 to 1832 Enos T. Throop was the state's chief executive. Throop's old home, Willowbank, a rambling brown structure built in 1818, with large stables and behind a stockade fence, still stands on the east side of Owasco Lake near its foot. There a descendant of the governor, Edward S. Martin, first editor of Life magazine, lived as a boy.

On a wall of the Cayuga County Court House is a tablet honoring an Auburnian who never held office, who could not even vote but who struck as heavy blows against slavery as ever Seward did.

Harriet Tubman was born a slave on Maryland's Eastern Shore. She escaped and went back to bring the rest of her family out of bondage. Before the Civil War she led 300 others to freedom. There was a reward on her head and incensed slaveholders kept increasing the sum. She was a leader in the Underground Railroad and her home was a station on the line of which she once said: "On the Underground Railroad I nebber run my train off de track and I never los' a passenger." She was the friend of John Brown, of Frederick Douglass and of William Lloyd Garrison.

During the Civil War Harriet Tubman served as a Union spy in the rebel lines, wearing men's clothing. She led 700 of her people away from the plantations and most of the men joined the Union army. She braved fire on the battlefields. She nursed and fed soldiers and fugitives, both black and white. She died in Auburn in 1913 at the age of 92, venerated as "the female Moses" and "the Joan of Arc" of her race. "Aunt Harriet's" old home at the end of South Street, where she housed and fed the indigent of her people, is to them a shrine.

* * *

After the Erie Canal was completed and Auburn was left high and dry, a canal was projected to link Owasco Lake with the Clinton Ditch. The first step was the building of a big dam at the foot of the lake in 1835. The project was financed by private capital and the state, which wanted the Outlet cleared to provide greater water power for the prison shops, helped build long stone piers across the sand bar at the old mouth of the Outlet. A new channel was dug in 1854, creating the present "island," the site of an amusement park for 65 years.

The big dam is still there but the ditch never was dug. In

its place came the Iron Horse. In 1838 the Syracuse and Auburn Railroad was opened and three years later Auburn was linked to Rochester by the rails. The railroad is still known as "The Auburn Road." In 1869 the Southern Central tracks were laid along the west shore of Owasco Lake to link Sayre, Pa. with Fair Haven, then a busy Lake Ontario port. Now it is a part of the Lehigh Valley system. It carries only freight but once it hauled many a long excursion train.

Those were the days of the picnics and the single sculling races at Elsenore, with its famous glen and its big Glen Haven Hotel, long gone from the scene; of the heyday of Cascade at the head of the lake and of the eight-oared barge, the Dolphin, and the Dolphin Association's club house on the east shore. Those days are vividly recalled by Maj. Wheeler C. Case, a native of Auburn, now a resident of Rochester, in his booklet, "Along Owasco Water."

On September 27, 1877, more than 20,000 people flocked to Elsenore. They came in 80 excursion coaches of the Southern Central which ran special trains from Auburn and Moravia, in buggies and carriages and on foot. It was the day of an epic single sculling race and the crowds saw Charles E. Courtney of Union Springs, later Cornell's celebrated rowing coach, win over James Riley, "Frenchy" Johnson and James Ten Eyck.

Owasco had its steamboat era and it was a pleasant one. They plow the lake only in memory now—the Owasco, the propeller-driven Elsenore, the Moravia, the Lady of the Lake and the broad-beamed City of Auburn. On a wall in the Museum of History at Auburn hangs a long piece of polished wood. It is highly treasured for on it is the name "The Lady of the Lake."

Auburn gentry, among them the Sewards, the Osbornes and Cases, built rather elaborate "camps" along the lake. Many of them went up in the 1880s and are still in the families of their builders.

On the east shore of Owasco Lake lives one of America's foremost writing men, Samuel Hopkins Adams. He lives on land that belonged to his Grandfather Hopkins and as a boy he learned to sail and swim in Owasco Lake. On its shores he has turned out much of his prodigious literary grist. He is the author of a score of books and of countless magazine articles. You can hardly pick up a magazine these days, it seems, without noting an article from his typewriter. He is a most remarkable man. For Samuel Hopkins Adams, loyal and articulate son of Owasco, was born in 1871.

Millard Fillmore is probably the least remembered of our Presidents. But around the old village of Moravia, south of Owasco's shores, he is not forgotten. In Moravia's St. Matthew's Episcopal Church there's a tablet commemorating his marriage there to Abigail Powers and a marker at the site of his log cabin birthplace at Summer Hill, although few go there nowadays.

Many more visit the 400-acre Fillmore Glen State Park, one mile south of Moravia. It is a place of rugged natural beauty. There Fall Creek, etching its path through the rocks, plunges over five waterfalls. At the foot of the main falls is a strange rock formation called "the Cowpens." The pool there is a popular neighborhood bathing place.

Few of our Presidents had a more humble beginning than

Fillmore. His parents were wretchedly poor. He had to go to work at a tender age. Self taught, he got a job teaching school. He studied law and moved to the booming city of Buffalo where he entered politics. He became Thurlow Weed's lieutenant in the western part of the state and went to Congress. In later years he broke with Weed and Seward and swung over to Henry Clay. He was put on the Whig ticket with Zachary Taylor in 1848 as a sop to the disgruntled Clay forces.

He was a big, full-featured man of urbane manners and he made an impressive figure presiding over the Senate as Vice President. Then one day in 1849 old Zach Taylor ate too many cherries and drank too much cold milk after standing too long in the hot sun during the dedication of the Washington Monument and Millard Fillmore, born in a log cabin, moved into the White House.

His reign was undistinguished and marred by compromise and he was denied a renomination. He was an affable middle-of-the road politician who aroused neither passionate devotion nor fierce enmity. Historians have not been kind to Millard Fillmore. One of them called him "a bland nonentity." But the Finger Lakes Country can't let him down. He was its only native son who ever made the White House.

*　　*　　*

Four miles northwest of Moravia on the east side of Owasco Lake is one of those blue historical markers you see all over the Lakes Country. This one marks the site of the frame house, long since burned down, where John D. Rockefeller, Sr., the oil magnate and once the richest man in the world, lived as a boy.

His family came there when he was four years old and lived there six years. In later years the oil king recalled sleeping with his brother, William, on the top floor of the farmhouse, heated only by a stove pipe. He earned his first money in a characteristic way—by stalking a turkey hen, finding its nest, taking its baby chicks and raising and fattening them for market. When he was an old, old man John D. made a pilgrimage to the scenes of his youth and scattered dimes among the villagers at Moravia.

About his father, William Rockefeller, hangs an air of mystery. "Big Bill" was a flamboyant figure, powerfully built, virile, and he had a way with women. He cut quite a dash in the neighborhood with his flashy rigs and fast horses. Once he had been a peddler of patent medicine. He lived on farms but he never did much real farming. Horseflesh was his first love. He never lived long in one place and to this day, down Moravia way, the natives will tell you that "Big Bill came in the night and left in the night."

In 1927 a curious little book was published. Its author was a Charles Brutcher and its title was "Joshua, A Man of the Finger Lakes Region," purporting to be "A True Story from Real Life." It is a rare volume today.

The hero is "Joshua Rosecamp." Its villain is Joshua's neighbor, given the name of "William Rockwell." It is a rambling, dramatic tale. It relates strange goings-on at the Rockwell place, of a secret cave in the hills that was the rendezvous of a gang of horse thieves; of a gully, reached by a hidden path, where of nights horses neighed and lanterns glowed. In the end Rockwell is pictured fleeing Auburn with ten jurymen at his heels after a trumped up charge against Joshua blows up in the Cayuga County Court House.

In his preface the author states that "William Rockwell was the father of John, who was destined to become one of the world's most powerful business men," and that "this story was inspired by Joshua Rosekrans—who related this story to his son, Melvin, to be confirmed later by a number of old settlers from Cayuga County. . . . Melvin Rosekrans was instrumental in compiling this book."

I met one of the Rosekrans clan at Fillmore Glen State Park. He insisted the story of "Joshua" was the Gospel truth. So did many others in the Owasco Lake region.

It all happened a long time ago, in a rough frontier time. Unquestionably there was a lot of horse stealing going on in those days. There was a "Horse Underground Railroad" and traces of its stockades still remain. Horses were stolen below Mason's and Dixon's Line and brought back to York State to be sold.

When the "Underground" began operating in both directions and missing York State horses showed up in Dixie, Upstaters girded for battle, formed vigilance committees and broke up the gangs.

*　　*　　*

Into the industrial history of Auburn is woven the story of most of her leading families and also of their impressive bequests to their city.

Manufacture of farm equipment along the Owasco began

in 1818 with a scythe plant that lasted a long time. In 1858 David M. Osborne began manufacture of a combined reaper and mower invented by an Auburnian named Kirby. In the beginning the Osborne plant had only 12 employes. It grew into one of the nation's biggest farm machinery plants and in 1903 was merged into the International Harvester Company. In 1950 Auburn ceased to be "the Harvester City" when the International closed its works. It seemed a heavy blow at the time but since then new industries, notably a General Electric Company electronics plant, have closed the breach.

All over Auburn you run into the name, Osborne. There is an Osborne Street and the leading hotel, the plushy old downtown hostelry that has seen so many banquets, conventions and political deals, still bears the Osborne name and is still in the family. Three generations of Osbornes, David M., Thomas Mott and Charles D., have been mayors of Auburn. Charles D. and his brother, Lithgow, are influential citizens, with newspaper and industrial interests, as well as being leading Democrats. Lithgow Osborne, former state game commissioner and minister to Norway, has been mentioned as gubernatorial timber.

Auburn's City Hall is the gift of two daughters of D. M. Osborne as a memorial to their father. The city police station also is an Osborne gift. The imposing building housing the Women's Educational and Industrial Union was made possible by Mrs. Elizabeth W. Osborne in 1907.

Auburn is sometimes called "The Cordage City." Its Columbian Cordage plant is said to be the second largest in the world. It was organized in 1903 by Col. Edwin D. Metcalf to make binding twine for Osborne harvesters.

For 85 years shoes have been made in Auburn. The Enna Jettick brand is nationally known. A shoe manufacturer, Fred L. Emerson, gave Emerson Park at the foot of the lake to his city.

The name of Case is an outstanding one in the world of science. Willard E. Case gave up his law practice to become a scientific investigator and writer. His papers were read before the Royal Society of London. He established the Case Laboratories where his son, Theodore W. Case, perfected the tube that made possible the sound movies. The Case family donated the Victorian mansion in South Street that now houses the Cayuga County Museum of History. It contains many relics of Indian and pioneer times, including the original patent granted Jethro Wood of Moravia Falls for devising the first cast iron plow. He got only patent litigation for his pains. The building housing the Seymour Public Library was a Case family bequest. The library was donated by James Seymour, a locomotive manufacturer.

So the story runs. Auburn millionaires—and they have been numerous—have given generously to the city where they made their fortunes.

Most of Auburn's 46 diversified industries are long established ones. You sense that here is no "Johnny Come Lately" town, despite its industrial tempo. There is an air of long-standing stability about this city at the crossroads, with a thick layer of conservatism. It was not until after the turn of the century that the peoples of Southern and Eastern Europe came, to make it something of a melting pot.

Among the notable names that sprinkle the pages of the city's annals are those of:

Raymond Hitchcock, the actor, born in Auburn in 1865; William Seward Burroughs, inventor of the adding machine who began his career as a bank clerk in Auburn; William G. Fargo, co-founder of a great express company, once an agent at the old Auburn Road depot; William Miller Collier, diplomat and Peace Conference consultant after World War I, long an Auburn resident; Albert H. Hamilton, criminologist and microscopic expert, a witness in some famous court trials.

There are some old houses around Auburn whose bricks were laid and whose timbers were sawed by a young artisan who lived in the region in the 1820s. His name was Brigham Young and the first of his 27 wives was Miriam Works of Aurelius.

Since the days of Throop and Seward, Auburn's politicos have been influential ones. For 30 years white mustached Sereno Elisha Payne, of portentous bulk and innate conservatism, served in Congress. He specialized in the erection of high tariff walls and was Speaker Cannon's righthand man when "Uncle Joe" bossed the House. In later years America has become familiar with the booming voice of Representative John Taber of Auburn, raised ever in the interests of economy—and more economy.

For many years Auburn was the virtual capital of the minor baseball leagues of America. It was the headquarters of Auburn's John H. Farrell, a onetime messenger boy, who as secretary-treasurer of the National Association of Professional Baseball Leagues, ran the minor league show.

Twenty years ago Auburn's Steve Halaiko, amateur United States lightweight boxing champ who turned pro, was a big one in the world of fisticuffs.

And in 1935 the man mountain, Primo Carnera, trained at Auburn's Island Park for his fight with Joe Louis, which the Negro won.

Auburn is the city of cordage, celebrities and of Copper John—and a whole lot more. And the sparkling Finger Lake at its southern door is worth going a few miles out of your way to see.

Chapter 4

"Far Around Cayuga's Waters"

Cayuga is an old Indian name which is translated as "boat landing." "Long blue streak" would be more aptly descriptive.

For Cayuga is the longest of the Finger Lakes—40 miles of moody water from its head which nestles among mighty hills only some 40 miles from the Pennsylvania line to its foot which strokes the marshlands only 35 miles from Lake Ontario.

It has a maximum width of two miles and a maximum depth of 435 feet. It is 381 feet above sea level and it bends gracefully toward the west from its southern tip.

It's "far around Cayuga's waters" in time as well as in distance. On its only island scientists have found the remains of a people who lived there 5,000 years ago. More historical markers line its shores than those of any of its sister lakes.

They tell the sites of ancient towns of the Cayuga Nation, of missions where priests raised the cross in the 17th century, of the camps of Sullivan's army in the raid of 1779, of long vanished pioneer settlements, of landings where a steamboat has not docked in half a century, of a bridge that once was the longest in the Western world, of the cradle of women's suffrage and the birthplace of the bloomer.

The ghosts of the past walk through a scenic wonderland that is timeless. Man has preserved it and made it more ac-

46

cessible. In one of the four state parks around Cayuga Lake is a waterfall higher than Niagara. The scenic splendor around its rugged head really merits the extravagant title of "The Switzerland of America."

Amid the distant drums of history and the music of falling waters throbs the pulse of modern life. At the head of the lake is a distinctive city of 30,000, Ithaca, seat of mighty Cornell University. At its northern gate is Seneca Falls, a village of 7,500 that really is a lively little city. There is another college "far above Cayuga's waters" besides Cornell. It's serene little old Wells College at Aurora.

Around Cayuga Lake is a countryside of diversified agriculture, with dairying predominating at the south and fruit raising to the north. Table salt is pumped from the lake and rock salt mined from the bowels of the earth at Cayuga's southeastern corner.

The story of Ithaca and Cornell, the blend of "town and gown" at the head of the long blue lake, will be told in a later chapter. This one will deal with the lake itself and the other communities "far around Cayuga's waters."

*   *   *

In the early days Cayuga Lake was a busy pathway of commerce. From Ithaca and other ports the steamboats and the barges hauled the lumber, potash, plaster and other products of the frontier.

Since 1828 Cayuga Lake has been a part of the state's Seneca-Cayuga Canal, 90 miles long and a link with Seneca Lake and the Erie Canal. Its traffic is pretty slim nowadays. Once it was considerable.

That was in the era of the steamboats which began in 1819 with the launching of the Enterprise, first steamer on the Finger Lakes. By 1836 there were three others, the Telemachus, the De Witt Clinton and the Simeon De Witt. In 1850 the first modern passenger steamboat, the Kate Morgan, ushered in the excursion era. Then came a long list that included the Howland, the Forest City, the Beardsley, the Sheldrake, the Aurora, the Ithaca alias the T. D. Wilcox, the Ino, the Iroquois, the Mohawk and the Frontenac.

The name of the Frontenac calls to mind a great tragedy. On July 27, 1907, the 37-year-old double-decked side wheeler which had been plying the lake for 25 years, steamed northward from Ithaca on its daily run with 60 passengers aboard. A 50-mile gale was whipping up the lake.

As the boat left Aurora docks, people on shore noticed a wisp of flame around its smokestack. They shouted after the receding boat but the wind drowned their cries. In the bay off Farley's Point near Union Springs the fire was discovered. The gale had spread the flames so that the engineer could not reach the pumps and the life boat could not be lowered. Crew and passengers leaped into seven feet of choppy water. Nine of them, seven women and two children, were drowned and the Frontenac ran aground and died in a crackle of flames and a cloud of smoke. Summer people manned boats and made some heroic rescues.

On April 15, 1925, the Col. J. H. Horton, a little steamer which served the cottage colony at the head of the lake, burned at its dock—without any loss of life. Its passing wrote finis to more than a century of steamboating on Cayuga Lake.

Seneca Falls is two miles from Cayuga water at its nearest point but the historic industrial village is the gateway from the north and the west to the lake that has always been its playground.

Seneca Falls owes its existence and its name to a 50-foot waterfall in the Seneca River. The Seneca Turnpike brought its early settlers. It has always been on the main road across the state.

Its first permanent settler, Lawrence Van Cleef, was a resolute character. He first saw the Lakes Country as a soldier with Sullivan and returned in 1790 as a settler. Four years after he had built a log house on land he thought was his, he learned that he had been cheated and that his title was invalid. Furthermore the tract was to be put up for sale by the state. With $1,800 in his pockets, Van Cleef walked all the way to Albany. He arrived too late. A land syndicate had grabbed his tract for $2,000. Undaunted, he obtained another site and built a tavern and the first frame dwelling in the settlement upon it.

It was the water power of the Seneca River that attracted the four wealthy gentlemen who made up the Bayard Company. For a quarter of a century that land syndicate controlled the water power and the settlement that grew up around the falls. Col. Wilhelminus Mynderse arrived as agent for the syndicate and became an important figure in the village. He built a grist mill and a store at the falls where the combine charged a fee for portage.

The village became a way stop for the stage coaches and settlers' wagons rolling over the turnpike. But it did not really flourish until after the monopolistic land company dissolved in 1827 and the state, taking over the water rights, built the Cayuga-Seneca Canal, paralleling the river. The canal boats brought life and color, as well as commerce to the village. Flour mills rose on its banks. Some of the old stone mills are there today.

By 1840 the village could boast a population of 4,200. Its industry was concentrated along the river and the canal and on the islands between them—until 1915. That year, the state, as a part of its grandiose Barge Canal scheme, canalized the Seneca River at Seneca Falls. The falls gave way to a dam and twin locks, with a power plant adjoining. The "industrial islands" were wiped out by the union of the canal and the river. Of that marriage was born the pretty little lake, in the heart of the village only a few steps from the busy roar of Fall Street's traffic, just east of the tall flag pole. Some folks call it "the million dollar lake." It gives the village a picturesque touch and Trinity Episcopal Church a setting few religious edifices possess. Only an occasional oil barge and a few pleasure craft go through the locks these days.

The lake and the park bear the name of pioneer Van Cleef. You find the names of Van Cleef and Mynderse all over the village. On the shores of Van Cleef Lake is Mynderse Library. The village high school through the years has retained its old name of Mynderse Academy. And in Van Cleef Park is a bandstand that was the gift of a man who bore both hallowed names, Mynderse Van Cleef.

And they say that when the waterway is drained to permit repair of the locks, "the lost islands" reappear, with the ghostly foundations of old plants and warehouses and the outlines of long buried streets at the bottom of the lake.

Only the tablet on its wall makes the auto sales room at Fall and Mynderse Streets with its modern front different from the rest of the business blocks. But if you look closely at the building's old brick rear with the high windows, there are the outlines of the old Wesleyan Chapel.

It is a historic building. It is the Independence Hall of feminine America. There on July 19 and 20, 1848, the first women's rights rally in the nation was convened. A leader in that historic assemblage was a young matron of Seneca Falls, Elizabeth Cady Stanton.

The story goes back to 1840 and the world anti-slavery convention in London, England. In its American delegation were Mrs. Stanton and Mrs. Lucretia Mott, a Philadelphia Quakeress of advanced views. The two women were barred from the proceedings and forced to sit behind a screen, shut off from public gaze. It was a man's world in 1840.

Stung by the indignity, Mrs. Stanton and Mrs. Mott discussed calling an equal rights convention on their return to America. They kept up a correspondence but took no definite action until the early Summer of 1848, when Mrs. Mott came to Auburn to visit her sister, Mrs. Martha Wright. She called on Mrs. Stanton in nearby Seneca Falls. Out of that reunion grew the call for a convention to proclaim a new status for women. Sitting around a table in the Waterloo home of Quaker Richard Hunt, five women, Mrs. Stanton, Mrs. Mott, Mrs. Wright, Jane Hunt and Mary Ann McClintock drew up the notice of the meeting which appeared in the Seneca County Courier.

On the appointed day a crowd gathered at the Wesleyan Chapel. There were some men among the crowd and although the first session had been advertised "for women only," it was decided to admit the men. One of them, Frederick Douglass, the Negro leader then publishing an Abolitionist paper in Rochester, seconded Elizabeth Stanton's keynote resolution.

The women drew up a ringing declaration of independence after the man-made 1776 model. By resolution they demanded the right to free education, equality with men in business and the professions, the right of free speech and to participate in public affairs and the right to vote. All but the last named were adopted unanimously.

The rebels held another meeting, on August 2 in Rochester, and amid a howl of national derision from press and pulpit, the 81-year-long battle for equal suffrage began. The Seneca Falls convention of 1848 was "the Lexington and Concord" of that revolution.

Elizabeth Cady Stanton lived in the village until 1861. All her long life she fought for the cause. Her old home still stands in Washington Street. It—and the auto sales room that was the Wesleyan Chapel—were the centers of ceremonies marking the centennial of the women's rights movement held in the village in 1948.

Living in Seneca Falls at the time of the women's right rally but not a leader in its deliberations was slight, spare, 30-year old Amelia Jenks Bloomer, wife of a lawyer-publisher-politician. She was an ardent worker for temperance. Mrs. Stanton interested her in the equal rights movement. In 1849 Mrs. Bloomer began publishing a little magazine, devoted mostly to the temperance cause. She called it the Lily.

That year Mrs. Elizabeth Smith Miller, daughter of Gerrit Smith, the abolitionist-reformer, came from Geneva to visit her friend, Mrs. Stanton, in Seneca Falls. Mrs. Miller wore a strange new costume, short skirts and Turkish trousers. Mrs. Stanton also donned the as yet unnamed costume and the two women wore the garb on the streets of Seneca Falls, creating something of a sensation, even in a village used to unconventional female doings.

Mrs. Bloomer wrote an article in her magazine describing the costume. Other publications copied it and editors all over the nation commented, generally derisively, on the newest quirk of rebellious womanhood. Thus the name of Amelia Bloomer of Seneca Falls became forever attached to the garment which she did not originate, was not the first to wear— but which she only publicized. Posterity knows her as the First Bloomer Girl.

While the women were putting Seneca Falls in the spotlight with their suffrage rallies and their bloomers, its men were quietly pioneering in industry—with pumps and fire engines.

Since 1840 wooden pumps had been made in the village. Then John Cowing devised an iron pump and Seabury Gould began making iron pumps in a factory along the river in 1850. That was the start of the Gould Pump Company, one of the largest in the world. The business has always been in the Gould family. The present head is Norman J. Gould, who was a Republican Congressman of national prominence from 1915 to 1923. For many years the Rumsey Company also made pumps in Seneca Falls. The old Rumsey plant beside the canal locks now houses the Sylvania Electric works, a considerable enterprise.

For many years Seneca Falls was a center of fire engine manufacturing. The first engines were equipped with a rotary pump invented by Birdsall Holly, who later moved to Lockport and fathered a widely used water system for municipalities. Once the Silsby and La France fire engines, made in Seneca Falls, were used all over the world.

The village now produces, along with pumps, yarn, rulers, machine tools and other goods. Seneca Falls has the never-say-die spirit of its first settler, Van Cleef. If an industry departs, it goes out and gets another.

From the industries that flowered in the 19th Century stem the big houses, mostly brick Victorian, that line shady Cayuga Street on the north side of the river. On the south side, in the older residential section, is one of the most distinctive residences in the Finger Lakes region. It is the gray stone house built more than a century ago by Judge Gary V. Sackett, a pioneer canal promoter. Long stone steps lead up to an exquisite old doorway, which, with green blinds, fan windows, basement apartment in the Southern fashion, reflect the dignified taste of another day. The building is now the home of the Knights of Columbus.

*   *   *

Swinging down Cayuga's west shore, we come upon Cayuga Lake State Park, three miles from Seneca Falls, and with its beaches, picnic grounds, golf course and sylvan setting a playground for the area.

At nearby Canoga a monument marks the birthplace of the orator, Red Jacket. The present Canoga village is on the site of an Indian Canoga village. The name means "place of the floating oil." The Cayuga town was destroyed by a detachment of Sullivan's men, 200 strong under Colonel Dearborn, which in September of 1779, left the main army at Kanadesaga (Geneva) and laid waste the Indian country on the west shore of Cayuga Lake. In a treaty of 1795 the Indians reserved a mile-square plot around their old village for the use of a chief with the name of Fish Carrier. The reservation was abandoned in a few years.

Between Cayuga and Seneca Lakes but nearer Cayuga is the village aptly named Interlaken. But that has not always been its name. It lived under the various names of Farmerville, Farmer Village and Farmer until the Lehigh Valley built a new station there in 1904. The railroad wanted a fancier name than Farmer, and Interlaken, after the Swiss town in another lakes country, was chosen. Interlaken long has been a trading center for the countryside and for summer people on the lake.

Only eight miles from the head of the lake is the village of Trumansburg. Its name has no connection with the present occupant of the White House. Its first settler was Abner Treman, the first of many Tremans in Tompkins County. He came in 1792 and the place took his name. When he was made its first postmaster, the official who made out the commission misspelled the postoffice name and Trumansburg it has remained.

Above the lake and about two miles west of the old village of Jacksonville, Nature stages a grand and endless spectacle. There in the state park of the same name, the silvery waters of Taughannock Falls plunge down 215 feet in an amphitheater whose rocky walls are 300 feet high. The falls are 30 feet higher than Niagara and are the highest straight falls east of the Rockies. The scene is breath-taking.

About its name hovers an old Indian legend. Once a chief of the Onondagas branded the Delawares cowards for selling their lands in Pennsylvania to the whites. To avenge the insult, a young chief of the Delawares named Taughannock led a force of 300 braves against the Onondagas. At Taughannock Falls the Delawares were crushed by a superior force and all but two of them were killed. Taughannock's bravery so impressed his foes that they named one of the grandest natural spectacles in the East in his honor.

Southwest of the lake are two other state parks. Robert H. Treman Park, named after its Ithaca donor, is 850 acres of wild and rugged beauty. Lucifer Falls in its upper section is 115 feet high. In the lower park are Enfield Falls and Glen, a fine swimming place.

Two miles south of Ithaca on the Elmira road is 350-acre Buttermilk Falls State Park. There Buttermilk Creek drops more than 500 feet in a "one-way escalator" of cascades and rapids through awe-inspiring gorges.

Six miles south of the park and also on the Elmira road, amid towering hills, stands a lone survivor of a day that will never return. In Newfield Village is the only covered bridge left in the Finger Lakes country. There are less than 40 of them in the whole state and only one other west of Herkimer. That is near Cowlesville in Wyoming County.

The bridge at Newfield, painted red and sturdy and well

A Puff of Wind on Owasco Lake

Seneca Falls Waterfront

Taughannock Falls, Highest in the East

Cornell, "Far Above Cayuga's Waters"

kept, carries the village's Bridge Street over the west branch of the Cayuga Inlet, known locally as Newfield Creek. The 80-foot single span bridge, built in 1853, is maintained by the Town of Newfield and an object of great pride to the townspeople, particularly the small boys.

On its old timbers are the carved initials of swains and sweethearts, amid the tattered remains of signs advertising spavin cures, horse and cattle condition powders, vegetable pills, sewing machines and county fairs. At Newfield Bridge the horse and buggy days still live.

*   *   *

Around Cayuga Lake's southeastern corner in the Myers-Ludlowville area is a considerable salt industry. The International Salt Company pumps the salt-laden water from the lake and separates the brine through evaporation. The rock salt mines of the Cayuga Salt Company nearby are 2,000 feet down in the earth.

On the eastern shore at South Lansing is Rogue's Harbor, made famous by Ithaca novelist Grace Miller White's book, "Judy of Rogue's Harbor." The old hotel in which some of her scenes were laid is still there. It was also on a farm near Rogue's Harbor back in the 1850s that the scholarly rogue, Edward Ruloff, supposedly murdered his wife and child, although the crimes were never proved because there were no corpses. Later neighbors remembered a mysterious box that was hauled away on a Ruloff wagon. Ruloff was tried twice in Ithaca Court House but was convicted only of abduction. The case was a sensation of the time. Later the Jekyll-Hyde character of the Finger Lakes wound up on the gallows as the result of a holdup-slaying in Binghamton.

The name of John King and the ferry he ran in pioneer days in conjunction with his tavern on the lake is perpetuated in the village of King Ferry, a few miles inland and surrounded by large Seckel pear orchards.

About midway up the eastern shore is the serene old village of Aurora, seat of Wells College and rich in history and lore. In 1779 a detachment of 600 troops of Sullivan's army under Col. William Butler laid waste the Indian village of 14 log houses on the site.

Aurora, first settled in 1786, won the Cayuga county seat away from Cayuga Village in 1799, only to lose it to up-and-coming Auburn ten years later.

The lakeside village has been a college town since 1868—because Henry Wells, the express magnate, lived there. Wells, a native of Vermont, came to the region in 1814 at the age of 9. In his youth he worked on farms and in a cobbler shop at Port Byron. He started his express career by carrying parcels in a small hand bag. He traveled from Albany to Auburn by rail, thence by stage to Geneva, and by rail and stage to Buffalo. The trip took four days in Summer and much longer in Winter. The postal authorities fought him in the courts. The people along the line sided with the express messenger and some toll gatekeepers closed their gates on the mail carriers and let Henry Wells through. In the end the express man was upheld in the courts.

Later Wells joined forces with William G. Fargo and they extended their lines to the West, founding the American Express Company and later the company that bore their names.

Fargo went to live in a stylish mansion in Buffalo but Henry Wells stayed on in little Aurora in his stately stone house, Glen Park, that is now a part of Wells College.

In 1868 he founded Wells Seminary for the Higher Education of Young Women as a non sectarian liberal arts school. It was the second women's college in the state (Vassar is older by five years). In 1870 it changed its name to Wells College.

Wells College's 345-acre campus, sliding from a lofty summit down to the lake, is picturesque. Adjoining it is Payne Creek gully, also known as Moonshine with its Moonshine Falls and shadowed by strange-shaped Pumpkin Hill. The college buildings are a blend of the new and the old. The library is named after one of the most famous of Wells graduates, "Frankie" Folsom of the class of 1885, who married Grover Cleveland.

Wells draws its students from many states. Its traditions are democratic. The girls draw lots for their rooms and a girl from one of the wealthiest families during her whole college career chanced to have one of the poorest rooms. The present enrollment is around 300, in a village of 200.

The college barn houses a genuine Wells-Fargo coach used in the West in frontier times. Every May Day and Commencement it is hauled out, along with an old horse-drawn bus that once plied New York's Fifth Avenue and the cumbersome old vehicles are filled to their roofs with white-clad college girls. The villager who drives the Wells-Fargo coach is likely to be wearing a top hat, a frock coat and rubber boots, hardly an authentic costume of the plains.

The last of the Morgans died recently in Aurora. The

family for 150 years was a leading one in the region. One of the clan, Lewis Henry Morgan, went to live in Rochester, where he attained eminence as an anthropologist and an authority on Iroquois lore. As a boy he picked up a lot of that lore visiting the Cayuga tribes in the hills around Aurora. Edwin B. Morgan was the first president of Wells-Fargo and helped Henry Wells found his seminary. A later Edwin Morgan was a distinguished diplomat.

A pleasant place is Aurora with its college-owned, 118 year-old inn by the lake, its serene and sylvan campus on the hillside, its main street flanked by lovely old homes.

Every community on the eastern shore is a historic one. Two miles east of little Levanna remains of an ancient people, probably Algonkian, were uncovered some years ago. They included effigies of a bear, a panther, a thunder bird and other sacred animals. On the northern edge of Levanna is the stone house, Ingleside, which according to tradition, Washington Irving built for his niece and her husband, W. R. Grinnell, and where the creator of Rip Van Winkle and Ichabod Crane spent some Summers. In this house, which has been added on to since Irving's time, was planned the expedition financed by Henry Grinnell in 1850 which failed by only a few degrees to reach the South Pole.

At Great Gully Brook, north of Levanna, once glowed the council fires of Cayuga Castle, capital of a nation. It was there, through a friendly chief, that the Jesuits, Menard and Chaumont in 1656 established the second Roman Catholic mission chapel in New York State. Fathers de Carhiel and Pierre Raffeix carried on the chapel until 1684. The Jesuits described the place "as the fairest ever seen" and wrote of "the chestnut and oak trees and the pigeon flocks that darkened the sky." A white cross and a wayside shrine mark the site of the pioneer mission.

Another white visitor to Cayuga Castle was Sir William Johnson, the lord of the Mohawk Valley, in the pre Revolutionary time when he was forging powerful ties between Britain and the tribes. During the Revolution some other white men visited the capital. They wore the buff and blue of Sullivan's army and they burned Cayuga Castle to the ground.

Union Springs, the largest eastern shore community, was settled in 1800 and Quakers were among its fathers. Once it claimed to have the largest plaster quarry in America. In early days when the plaster business flourished along Cayuga Lake, the stone was shipped by boat to Ithaca whence it eventually found its way to the seaboard. During the War of 1812 the United States commandeered 50 plaster boats at Union Springs for transporting invasion troops to Canada. The scheme fell through and the plaster boats were consumed in a mysterious fire.

Frontenac Island, a small green speck in Cayuga's blue off Union Springs, is one of two islands in the Finger Lakes. The other is tiny Squaw Island at the foot of Canandaigua Lake. In 1939 and 1940 a Rochester Museum expedition under Dr. William A. Ritchie, now state archeologist, uncovered the burial sites of an archaic people that lived on the isle at least 5,000 years ago.

It has been 94 years since a wagon rumbled over the planks of Cayuga Bridge, once the longest in the hemisphere. That bridge played its part in the development of the western part of the state. Once "West of Cayuga Bridge" meant the wild frontier.

When after the Revolution the pioneers cut the Genesee Road through the woods to connect the older Eastern settlements with the new Genesee Country, the northern tip of Cayuga Lake and the Montezuma marshes offered the only water obstacle to an almost straight route across the state.

So the pioneers built a bridge. The one and one eighth miles of wooden trestle was begun in 1797 and completed in 1800. It was built on mud sills and was considered an engineering marvel of the age. The bridge cost $25,000 and was paid for out of tolls. The fee of 25 cents for a man and horse was considered excessive in those days. Across a bridge just wide enough for three carts to pass, streamed a mighty tide of migration. In 1807 the mud sills collapsed under the battering of lake ice. It was rebuilt on wooden piers in 1812–13 and troops marched over it in the War of 1812. It was rebuilt again in 1833 and lasted until 1857.

At the eastern end of the Long Bridge, a settlement sprang up. It was called Cayuga and it had many taverns. It also had the first Cayuga County Court House, which consisted of six posts set in the ground with poles resting upon them and a brush roof covering the ensemble. It was built in 1789. Under the end of the Long Bridge was the county's first jail. It received its prisoners through a trap door. The western terminal of the Cayuga Bridge was at Bridgeport, east of Seneca Falls, now only a cluster of houses.

Before the bridge was built, John Harris in 1788 opened the first ferry service on the lake, from Cayuga to the present site of the state park on the west side. His ferry sometimes was propelled by a sail, otherwise by oar power.

Years ago Cayuga was widely known as the place by the Long Bridge. Now it is best known as the home of a huge feed concern, which maintains experimental poultry and cattle farms in the vicinity.

In the swamp country north of the lake and near the village of Montezuma stood a fortified town of the Cayugas where Father Rene Menard had a mission as early as 1657. A bridge honors the name of the brave Jesuit.

For miles north of the lake stretch the wild Montezuma marshes. There is a large national wildlife sanctuary where rare birds are safe from nimrods. The region has always been good duck hunting country.

In the great swamps many criminals, horse thieves and escaped Auburn Prison convicts among them, have found sanctuary. Those fever-laden marshes claimed the life of many an Irish digger when the Clinton Ditch was cut through the Montezumas in the 1820s.

In recent years many acres of the marshes have been reclaimed and converted into rich muckland on which prodigious crops are raised. Blueberries, ordinarily habitants of a more northerly clime, grow in the Montezuma bogs, the only ones within a radius of 50 miles.

This is a strange land north of Cayuga's waters. It is unlike the rest of the Lakes Country. It is a brooding and a mystical countryside, where the drumlins, knobby relics of the glacial age, cast their strange-shaped shadows, where strange birds cry—and giant mosquitoes drone through the air like Flying Fortresses.

Chapter 5

Town and Gown—Ithaca and Cornell

"Ithaca N. Y.—Education and Scenery."

Such is the slogan on the booklets handed out by the Ithaca N. Y. Chamber of Commerce. Certainly the city at the head of Cayuga Lake offers both education and scenery on a grand scale. But Ithaca is too complex a quantity to be reduced to any two-word formula, no matter how apt.

Although college students (over 9,000 from Cornell University and 1,000 from Ithaca College) comprise more than a third of its 30,000 population, Ithaca is more than just a college town.

It is also a historic county seat and a busy trading center. Not primarily an industrial city, it has important industries. It has been called "the agricultural capital of the Northeast." It is a distinctive, cosmopolitan community, this city of the many hills. In the infancy of the silent movies, it was a "little Hollywood." And not the least of Ithaca's claims to lasting fame is that of being the birthplace of the soda fountain concoction known as the sundae.

And despite a popular impression gained from the radio on crisp Autumnal Saturdays, there is more to Cornell than the chant of "Far Above Cayuga's Waters" and the charge of "The Big Red team."

Cornell is a big university but there are 40 larger in America. Its greatness does not lie in mere bigness. Cornell is great because for 83 years it has been a vast laboratory, pioneering in almost every conceivable field and always in the liberal tradition in which it was founded. Even across the seas Cornell is regarded as a symbol of freedom of thought and action in a free world.

As for scenery, the city and the college share a glory of waterfalls, gorges, glens and caverns, majestic hills and long blue lake. Ithaca and the Cornell campus are really one vast park. What other city has within walking distance of its business center three mountain streams rushing through deep gorges and plunging over waterfalls, one of them 140 feet high? And few will dispute the statement that Cornell's campus is the most spectacularly beautiful in America.

"Education and scenery?" Yes, and a whole lot more. The story of town and gown, of the city in the valley and the college on the hill that is a veritable city in itself are interwoven yet they are distinct. And it must not be forgotten that there was an Ithaca in the valley before ever a college tower rose against the sky on a distant hill.

* * *

Ithaca is a child of the Cayuga Nation, of the Sullivan Expedition and of the old capital city of Kingston-on-Hudson.

When Dearborn's troopers reached the head of Cayuga Lake in 1779, they found there a small Indian village in a clearing on the flats. They destroyed it and the standing corn in the fields.

Ten years later white settlers began planting corn in that

same clearing. In 1788, 11 men of Kingston, with two Delaware Indians as guides, explored the Cayuga Valley. The next year three of them, Jacob Yaple, Isaac Dumond and Peter Himepaw, returned and took up land at the foot of East Hill. Soon there was a little colony of 19, all from Kingston.

After the opening of the Military Tract, much of the Cayuga Valley came into the hands of Simeon De Witt, the state surveyor-general who has been credited with pinning the classical names on the region. He named the settlement at the head of Cayuga Lake Ithaca because it was in the town of Ulysses. Ithaca was the isle where lived Ulysses, legendary hero of the Greeks.

Mills were built beside the rushing waters of the Cascadilla, Fall and Six Mile Creeks and beside the more quiet Inlet which flowed through the flatlands. Cayuga Lake became an important commercial highway and Ithaca, hemmed in on three sides by great hills, a key shipping port.

The War of 1812 boomed the port town which until then had contained only 50 houses. When the shipment of gypsum, used in making fertilizing plaster, was cut off from Canada, the lime-laden shores of Cayuga Lake became the principal source of supply and Ithaca the major shipping point for plaster.

During the rough and roaring early days, a group of bluenoses, the Morals Society, sought to guard the morals of the town. The Moralists punished inebriates and other offenders by dousing them with water, stripping them and locking them in with hogs, and other penalties. Finally some of their victims retaliated by seizing four of the Moralists and giving them the same treatment. After that the Morals Society died on the vine.

Ever since Tompkins County was formed in 1818, Ithaca has been the county seat. The village was incorporated in 1821. Seven years later the opening of the Cayuga-Seneca Canal gave it a mighty shot in the arm. Steamboats began to ply the lake and stage coaches rolled up to the stately, white pillared Clinton House, built in 1832, and still on the scene. In 1834 the second railroad in the state, the Cayuga and Susquehanna, began running between Ithaca and Owego.

In the late Edward Hungerford's book, "Pathway of Empire," is an interesting paragraph about the railroad: "As Ithaca is hemmed in by tremendous hills in every direction, she found the location of a railroad up and out of her waterfront a most difficult matter. It was only overcome by the construction of two long inclined-ways, whereon the cars were raised and lowered by cables worked, first by horses, and then by stationary engines. . . . After six years the railroad discontinued using horses and after some years the steep inclined-ways were discontinued and a curious switch back device substituted. . . . If you miss the train out of the station, you can take a cab and easily catch it at the upper level of the switchback." You could in 1935 when the book was written but now the road carries only freight.

Things never came too easily for Ithaca. Always it had to fight its geographical isolation in the formidable hills. The panic of 1837 virtually bankrupted it. Fire and flood smote it. Vicissitudes beset its local industries. Ithaca rose above all its adversities and handicaps.

67

Destiny came to the town—on foot—in 1828 in the person of Ezra Cornell, a lanky, dark-haired, serious featured youth of 21. He walked the 40 miles from De Ruyter with a set of carpenter's tools over his shoulder and a few dollars in his pocket.

He was of Quaker stock, self reliant, stubborn and with mechanical skill in his hands and brain. He obtained work as a millwright and was given the job of overhauling some of the mills along Fall Creek. Water was diverted from a dam above 140-foot-high Ithaca Falls to the mills by a wooden flume down the south bank of the gorge. Sometimes the water would freeze and break the conveyor. Cornell ended that by digging a tunnel through the rock 200 feet long. His tunnel is still in use.

Ezra Cornell lost his job in the panic of 1837 and went over the country selling a patent plow, with little success. He helped build one of the first lines for the new "magnetic telegraph" and became financially interested in the telegraph venture. When Hiram Sibley of Rochester and others forced the consolidation of small competing lines, in some of which Cornell had stock, into the Western Union combine, a fortune in the form of a batch of Western Union stock was thrust on the Ithacan.

He went home, not realizing his good fortune. Then the Western Union dividends came rolling in and in 1863 he "had more money than he and his family needed" and began to use his income for the benefit of his fellow man. His first benefaction was the gift of $100,000 for the Cornell Public Library, which still functions in the heart of Ithaca.

His interest in farming had led him to assist in the founding of the state's first Agricultural College on Seneca Lake near Ovid. That college opened in December, 1860, but eleven months later closed its doors because nearly all the students and teachers marched off to the Civil War.

Then the Morrill Land Grant Act became law. Under its terms each state received a share of the public lands for the endowment of a college. The revenues from the lands were to carry the colleges.

Cornell and other trustees of the college at Ovid applied to the state legislature for the grant. The college on Seneca Lake had an empty building, a 440-acre farm and a mortgage of $70,000 on it. At the same time Senator Charles Cook sought the grant for the People's College which he had fathered in his home village of Havana, now Montour Falls, but which had not yet enrolled a single student. The People's College, which in later years became Cook Academy, got the grant—on the condition it raise $242,000. When it failed to do so, Cornell, then a state senator, proposed dividing the grant between the colleges at Ovid and Havana.

Serving in the Senate with him was Andrew D. White, a young, rich and cultured Syracusan who had his own ideas about a state university. Cornell University literally was born in his fertile brain. White opposed division of the land grant and urged Cornell, who had half a million dollars "more than he or his family would need," to establish a new college with the help of the land grant funds.

Cornell accepted the idea and offered the half million, and his 300-acre farm on a hill above Ithaca for the site. It was not his wish that the proposed school should have his name.

The bill embodying his offer in exchange for the land grant met bitter opposition. Denominational colleges did not like the idea of a non sectarian school and called it a "Godless institution." Others attacked the proposal as a "land grab." None was more virulent in opposition than Martin B. Anderson, president of the Baptist University of Rochester and the columns of the Rochester Democrat.

Senator White finally eased the bill through. He had to make some deals. One was mollifying the Ovid group by putting a state mental hospital on the old college site.

It was Ezra Cornell who supplied the money for the university and whose able handling of the public lands it received from the government put the college on a firm footing and gave it a steady income in the early days. But it was Andrew D. White who first proposed it and whose masterly campaign smoothed the way for its birth.

On Oct. 7, 1868, with that same Andrew White as its first president, Cornell University was opened on a hilltop that was mostly pasture land.

The launching of the "freshwater college" as some of its older contemporaries termed it, was chaotic. A total of 388 students poured in when only half that number had been expected. The only completed building on the campus, Morrill Hall, overlooked an open field. Cascadilla Place, a former water cure in which Ezra Cornell had been interested, was filled to the rafters with faculty and students. It was a combination dorm, dining room, office and about everything else. Old Cascadilla is still on the campus, still in the service of Cornell.

But there was nothing chaotic about the ideals of the infant college. Ezra Cornell stated them in these words that are still on the shield of the university:

"I would found an institution where any person can find instruction in any study."

The new college began with these basic principles, radical at that time: Emphasis on agriculture and the mechanical arts, the addition of history, political science and modern literature to the conventional liberal arts course and the granting to students more freedom in choice of studies and in conduct than was customary in that day.

Gradually other buildings rose around Morrill Hall. Some of the early ones were gifts of old associates of Ezra Cornell, hard headed business men such as Henry Sage, Hiram Sibley and the McGraw brothers.

Financial worries clouded the last years of Ezra Cornell. His college was on firm ground but his other enterprises, among them the network of railroads which he had fostered to guard his city against its isolation, fell into other hands. He died in 1874, a broken man.

The college on his old farmland on the hill had brought a cultural touch to the village of 7,000 in the valley that still was a little rough at the edges.

*   *   *

When it began in 1868, Cornell was swamped by its entering class of 388 students. Now there are more than 9,000, of whom 400 are from foreign lands. The ratio of men to women is about four to one. In 1868 the faculty numbered 26 professors and six of them were non residents. Among them were James Russell Lowell, George William Curtis,

Louis Agassiz and Bayard Taylor, "big names" for a fresh-water college.

In the beginning Cornell had two buildings. Now there are 90 on the campus at Ithaca. In 1868 the college's assets totalled $1,100,000 and that included the land grant. Its present endowment is 45 millions, exclusive of state grants; its property is valued at 42 millions and its overall budget is 36 millions of which more than one third is spent for research.

To describe in detail the layout of "the city on the hill" would require a book in itself. A campus guide of Cornell contains 160 pages. And not all of Cornell University is in Ithaca. There's the big Medical Center in New York City and the Aeronautical Laboratory in Buffalo. And the State Agricultural Experimental Station in Geneva is administered by Cornell.

Of its nine colleges, three are supported by the state. The rest are privately endowed. The names of millionaire donors are on its buildings, names like George F. Baker, Rockefeller, Myron C. Taylor and many more. The architectural hodgepodge on the campus reflects the various eras in which the gifts arrived.

Andrew Carnegie, who spent his last years giving away the millions he had struggled so hard to obtain, gave the filtration plant and made other donations. Once he was a Cornell trustee. Back in 1903 he made what was probably the only impulsive gift he ever made in his life. That winter a typhoid epidemic raged in Ithaca. Several students died and many more were stricken. Many of them were working their way and were in desperate straits because of lost wages during the period of illness and convalescence.

The bearded little Scottish steelmaster heard of their plight and sent a check, secretly, to defray the boys' doctor and hospital bills and to see them through until they could work again. It was not the biggest but it was the finest, most straight-from-the-heart endowment that ever came to Cornell.

Many trails have been blazed on the storied hill. In 1875 the first permanent outside electric arc lights in the world shone from the towers of the Chapel and McGraw Hall. They were powered by the first practical dynamo on the continent, built by a Cornell professor and a senior student. That dynamo may be seen today in Rockefeller Hall.

Cornell opened the first department of electrical engineering and the first school of nutrition in the nation. It pioneered in hotel management and its practice inn in Statler Hall, manned by students, is unique. The New York State School of Industrial and Labor Relations at Cornell is blazing a trail in a critical field.

Cornell scientists send out radio signals, hoping to contact the celestial bodies. They study the behavior of cosmic rays in a rock salt mine 2,000 feet below the surface of the earth at Myers. Three years ago they used for that experiment the old tunnel that Ezra Cornell had dug in the 1830s. They experiment with fruit tree sprays and fertilizers, with nuclear energy and racial relations. One student learns about artificial insemination in the bull barn while another struggles with the technique of mixing a Manhattan in the bar of the Statler Club.

The infinite scope of Cornell's explorations stirs the imagination. There is nothing jaded or cynical about this university and that is not entirely a matter of relative youth, but rather of the spirit. It was no coincidence that a Free World Youth Assembly was convened at Cornell last Summer while Communist youth were rallying in East Berlin. The wind that sweeps the hill above Cayuga blows fresh and free and clears the air of old taboos and tyrannies.

And there are the intangible things—the memories and the traditions that only the Cornellians know.

There are the revered names in the athletic Hall of Fame —Of Charles (Pop) Courtney and his great rowing crews and memories of the Lehigh observation trains that followed the crew races along the eastern shore and of Courtney's flaunting of the laws in dynamiting the Inlet ice in the early Spring that he might start training. There are the names of Jack Moakley and John Paul Jones, the miler; of Gloomy Gil Dobie and his years of undefeated gridiron glory, of George Pfann and there are memories of Big Red teams on old Percy Field, down the hill, before there was a Schoellkopf Field.

There are memories of cock fights downtown when the "townies" lined their champions up against the best of the hill—of the Dutch Kitchen and the initials carved on the walls and benches there—of the Alhambra and Zinck's and the song, "We'll all have drinks at Theodore Zink's"—of Renwick Park and Patsy Conway's Band—of debtor students' trunks hauled to the railroad stations at Ludlowville and Freeville to dodge the sheriff and his writs in the days of coonskin coats and flapping galoshes.

Those are those who remember when the Widow and the Sun, the campus journals, had such contributors as Kenneth Roberts and George Jean Nathan and a Dutch youth named Hendrik Willem Van Loon. There was a law student named George Rector in the class of '99, who made his first culinary experiments in a downtown furnished room in a battered saucepan over a gas jet—and surreptitiously, lest the landlord know.

In late years, as "Rym" Barry laments in his warmly nostalgic book, "Behind the Ivy," the city and the college have grown farther apart. As the campus became more and more a self sustaining community, there has been less and less need for students to go down the hill to the town that once "boarded, clothed and washed the Hill."

"Town and gown" relations at Ithaca have never been seriously strained. I have never seen headlines telling of riots or student mass battles with police in Ithaca. Of course there have been some overboisterous celebrations, some false fire alarms, some greasing of street car tracks on the hills and the like, but only one prank in recent years that resulted tragically and that was the death of a popular Negro chef through sophomoric introduction of chlorine gas into a frosh banquet.

On Saturdays in October and November Ithaca and all its environs are acutely aware of the presence of a college on the hill. An invasion of a city of 20,000 by 35,000 football fans crams the place to the rafters. But the jingle of cash registers is a pleasing sound.

Ithaca has never been afraid to try something new. Back in 1878 two years after the first telephone line had been constructed, there was a line running from the village (Ithaca did not become a city until 1887) to the campus. In 1885 when there were only 13 electric lines in the country, trolleys were running in State Street between the Lehigh Valley depot and the Ithaca Hotel. In 1893 while drivers of horse-drawn hacks looked on glumly, the street cars conquered the steep East Hill leading to Cornell.

Speaking of grades, those in Ithaca are the steepest, and there are more of them than in any other Upstate city of my acquaintance.

The hills that surround Ithaca, besides giving majesty to the landscape and giving residents the climbing agility of mountain goats, have made the city vulnerable to floods. There was a big one in the 1850's when Six Mile Creek went amuck. About every Spring the flats from Buttermilk to Hog Hole used to be awash and floating lumber and flapping pike were salvaged at the Fair Grounds. Ithaca was hard hit in the big flood of 1935, along with Watkins Glen and other places in deep valleys. Since then the creeks have been diked and other control measures taken. The recent trend of population has been to the heights around the city.

Ithaca cannot be classed as industrial but its factories have made a great diversity of products. One of the biggest industries is the Morse Chain plant which stands out like a fortress on South Hill.

In the late 1890s Everett Morse invented a spring for a two-wheeled cart and with his younger brother, Frank, began making them in a shop at Trumansburg. In 1898 they switched to the manufacture of a rocket joint chain for bicycles. After the bicycle fad waned, Frank Morse patented a high speed transmission chain which was important to the budding automobile industry. In 1906 the big plant was built in Ithaca. Morse made airplanes during World War I. Later on came adding machines and electric clocks. Now a subsidiary of a national auto parts concern, the plant is making power drive chains again.

Ithaca produces shot guns, adding machines, textiles, paper, machine tools, scientific instruments, leather goods. Its once important cement industry has departed.

For many reasons Ithaca wears the title of "farming hub of the Northeast." One, of course, is the presence of the State College of Agriculture at Cornell with its far flung extension services. The city houses the headquarters of the Grange League Federation, a powerful farm co-operative; the American Agriculturist, an important farm journal; State Farm Bureau Federation offices, a United States nutrition laboratory and other agencies allied to agriculture. And it is in the heart of a diversified farming region.

Ithaca College, which began life in 1892 as Ithaca Conservatory of Music, is no tiny school. It has an enrollment of over 1,000, and in any other city would not be so overshadowed by a mighty neighbor on a hill. The college buildings are grouped around De Witt Park downtown and it is a progressive school, with courses in music, speech, drama, radio and business.

That cooling concoction, the sundae, was born on a hot Sunday in 1891, hence the name. As the story goes, an Ithaca preacher came into C. C. Platt's drug store, weary and sweating after the Sunday morning service. He asked the druggist to fix a dish of ice cream and pour some syrup on it. Platt tried the dish on Cornell students. They liked it and spread the word—and thus another American institution was born.

*   *   *

Only a few middle-aged folk remember now the fabulous era when Ithaca was "Hollywood" before there was a California Hollywood.

It began in 1912 when Ted Wharton, a New York movie producer, came to film the Cornell-Penn game and was impressed by the scenery. At that time virtually all the pictures were being shot around New York City. The next Summer Wharton returned with two stars of the Essanay Company, Francis X. Bushman and Beverly Bayne, to make "Dear Old Girl of Mine" and other college screen romances, for which the Cornell campus was an ideal setting.

In 1915 the Wharton Studios leased Renwick Park (now the city's Stewart Park) and began making some of the pioneer serial thrillers. Some of the episodes of "The Perils of Pauline," featuring the fearless and shapely Pearl White, were filmed around Ithaca. Playing heavy roles with Pearl were Lionel Barrymore and Creighton Hale.

Movie making was primitive then by modern standards. The scriptless plot developed as the story moved along. Action was the thing. The gorges, waterfalls, the lake and the hills provided the natural backdrop. Ithaca residences and Cornell frat houses were borrowed for mansion scenes. So was furniture on occasion. A little ad in the Ithaca Journal would bring plenty of talent for the mob scenes.

Pearl White and her sisters of the serials were pushed off bridges, "drowned" in Cayuga Lake, strapped to buzz saws, saved from death in the nick of time from onrushing Lehigh trains. Bridges were blown up, street cars sent hurtling into Cascadilla gorge, papier mache ships sent to the bottom of the lake. It was an exciting time in Ithaca N. Y.

In 1916 the preparedness propaganda film, "Patria," was made in Ithaca with Irene Castle of dancing fame and Milton Sills as stars. In the cast was King Baggott, he of the white streak in his raven hair. International Films made the "Beatrice Fairfax" series at Renwick Park, with Olive Thomas as the heroine. Metro brought Norma Talmadge to the lot to play the leading lady in a sequel to "Tess of the Storm Country," a film adapted from the novel of the same name by Grace Miller White.

Ithaca's fabulous movie era ended in 1920. The Finger Lakes weather had not proved ideal for picture making and the industry moved West, out where Hollywood was bursting into full bloom in the golden sunshine.

Walking the streets of Ithaca today you see many middle aged business men, laborers, housewives, ordinary looking folk, who once were "in pictures" and have never forgotten it. Maybe they weren't stars but they were bit players, part of mob scenes, extras, film cutters, wardrobe mistresses, electricians, carpenters and the like.

In Ithaca they still talk about Pearl White, who was as colorful off stage as on. She smoked cigarets and wore slacks on the streets when ladies just didn't do that sort of thing and she drove her canary yellow Stutz Bear Cat at breakneck speed. Once Pearl was arrested for speeding in Trumansburg

79

and after the elderly justice of the peace had fined her $5, the siren of the serials flipped him a ten spot and a contemptuous "Keep the change. I am going out of this town a damn sight faster than I came in."

*   *   *

Once there was another city within the city, besides Cornell. They called it the "Silent City," although it could be noisy enough. Now the packing box shacks are gone from the cattails along the Inlet and the "Rhiners" who lived in them have long been scattered.

The squatter colony of the "Rhiners" was a hangover from the rough days of the canal. There few worked steadily. Mostly they fished and hunted and trapped. They fought and drank. Some of them did not marry. They just mated like the ducks they hunted in the swamps. They stole coal off passing freight trains.

The squatters went their uninhibited ways, scornful of disapproving city folks, of the police and of the First Ward Irish, their enemies in many a gang fight. Then Ithaca rigged up a game law forbidding the netting of fish. That was a major squatter "industry" and it dealt the colony a hard blow. Many "Rhiners" moved out but the rest stuck to their shanties at the head of the lake.

In 1925 the city played its trump card. It began buying through tax foreclosures the lands on which the "Rhiners" squatted and finally the last of the undesirables was ejected. The city of culture had won over the "Silent City." Now the old Glenwood Road, once cluttered with squatter kids and rubbish, bears the fancy name of Taughannock Boulevard and the squatter colony lives only in memories and in the novels of Grace Miller White whose father's farm was near the Inlet.

I don't know whether or not Mrs. White coined "The Storm Country" title for the Ithaca region. No mention is made of it in the Chamber of Commerce publicity. But it seems to fit. Like its education and its scenery, Ithaca's storms are generally on a grand scale.

But when the storm is over and the sun comes out, as it always does eventually, it shines on Ithaca's fascinating cosmopolitan swarm of sidewalk humanity. The bespectacled man in the quiet business suit may be a nuclear scientist from the Hill and he rubs elbows with a sunburned farmer in from Jacksonville or Hayt's Corners for a plow point, with a turbaned student from Bagdad, a Negro co-ed, a buxom housewife hurrying to the beauty shop who never forgets she played in a mob scene with Irene Castle in 1917, a brisk local business man, a workman from the Morse Chain plant and maybe even a long-deposed "Rhiner" or two.

Chapter 6

Seneca

LAKE OF THE HIDDEN GUNS

Seneca Lake is a lovely vixen.

Centuries ago the Red Men became enamored of its 36 miles of cold and shining water. They gave her the name of the mightiest nation of their confederacy. They made her wooded slopes where falling waters tinkled in the glens their happy hunting ground. But they never trusted her.

Seneca was not like her sister lakes. She seemed to be bottomless. She seldom was frozen over even in the coldest weather. She was given to gusts of temper and sudden tides that drove the war canoes on the rocks.

But she could be so charming when she smiled that the Red Men forgave her tantrums and her guile. And they held her in deepest awe, for supernatural voices spoke from her spring-fed depths—with the dull rumble of hidden guns.

The Senecas came to know other and more terrible guns along the lake—the cannon and flintlocks of Sullivan's men. After the invaders left, the Indian villages were wind-blown ashes, the crops were blackened embers, the orchards twisted ruin. In the War of the Revolution the Keepers of the Western Door lost their homeland forever.

Then Seneca Lake became a pathway of white man's empire. From 1788 until well into the 1830s a great tide of migration surged along the lake. Canals were dug to link the lakes and rivers and the products of the frontier flowed through a chain of inland waterways. The era of the canals passed. The railroads came and then the automobile to shove the picturesque old steamboats into oblivion.

Some once lively ports became drowsy hamlets. Geneva, at the foot of the lake, grew into a flourishing and distinctive city, the seat of two colleges. Watkins Glen at its head, with its wealth of natural splendor, became a mecca for tourists and a noted health resort. In between, the fecund countryside along its shores and on the ridges between the lakes lapsed into pleasant slumber.

Then the war drums sounded for the greatest conflict of all time, the second World War, and Seneca's quiet eastern shore awoke to find itself no longer a serene strip of farms and villages and summer cottages but the heart of a vast military reservation.

The old hamlet of Kendaia was blotted out and in its stead rose a huge munitions depot. To the north the lights of Sampson, a city of sprawling barracks, the second largest naval training station in America, housing 45,000 bluejackets, glittered in the sky.

Peace came and Seneca Ordnance Depot was retained. The naval station was abandoned and Sampson, after serving as a naval hospital, a commodities depot and a state college for GIs and rapidly falling into disrepair, was about to be converted into a state park when the Korean outbreak called it back into service—this time as an Air Force training base.

Again the impact of a faraway war struck the Seneca Lake

region and now in 1951 things are roaring again in the land of the lake guns.

There are those who live along the lake and scoff at the story of the uncanny drumming in its depths, saying "I have never heard them." Others will swear they have heard the sounds, variously described as thunder, drumming and popping, which they say is most pronounced at twilight, in the late Summer or early Fall and most distinct around Lodi Landing and Dresden. They will tell you, too, that the booming is loudest just before a disaster, as the flood of 1935.

The cannonading was very real to the superstitious Indians who read omens and portents into all the manifestations of nature. The mysterious thunder from the depths of this unpredictable lake—what did it mean? Maybe the God of Thunder was angry. Maybe an evil spirit dwelt in the lake that "had no bottom."

Around the lake guns is woven the legend of "The Wandering Chief." He was the young Agayenthah, tallest and bravest of the Seneca warriors. One June day when he was trailing a bear along the lake, a sudden electric storm drove him to seek refuge under a great tree at the edge of a cliff. Then came a blinding flash of lightning, an ear-splitting crash. The God of Thunder had dealt both chief and tree a fatal blow. Together they tumbled into the lake. Together they floated out on its surface.

The next day when storm clouds again gathered and the guns were calling, there drifted out on the bosom of the lake what appeared to be the trunk of a tree, erect and protruding out of the water. It floated slowly around the lake like a funeral barge. It was seen again and again, always in the deathlike stillness that precedes the storm. When the lake drums roll, people say "The Wandering Chief is on the march."

There is the legend of the Spirit Boatman, a spectral warrior paddling his canoe in the moonlight around the Painted Rocks at the southeastern corner of the lake near Watkins Glen. After the Sullivan invasion, crude images were found scrawled on the palisades there. The pictures were supposed to have told the story of a skirmish with the American army in which the Senecas were driven over the rocks. The journals of Sullivan's men give no hint of any such encounter. But the pictures are there on the rocks, whatever their origin and meaning may be.

Science has reared its learned head to explain the mystery of the lake guns. The wise men say the sound is caused by the popping of natural gas released from the rock rifts at the bottom of the lake. When the gas fields were developed around Tyrone in the 1920s, the boom of the Seneca Lake guns was fainter. After the short-lived field was exhausted, they resumed their wonted thunder.

But the Indians believe that the lake guns are sounding a requiem for the lost glory of the Keepers of the Western Door.

Because the lake has been frozen over nine times in recorded history, there is a modern legend that Seneca water placed in an automobile radiator, makes a sure fire antifreeze solution. Seneca's great depth, 618 feet, makes her one of the deepest inland bodies of water in the United States.

The story of navigation on Seneca Lake began in 1798 when amid the cheers of a multitude the sloop Alexander was launched at Geneva. It was one of the many promotions of Charles Williamson, land agent for a British syndicate that owned much of the present Western New York.

On Independence Day of 1828, the first steamboat churned the waters of the lake. It was the side wheeler, the Seneca Chief, which had been De Witt Clinton's flagship on his parade of triumph across the state that marked the opening of the Erie Canal.

Then came many steamboats, among them the Chemung, the Kanadesaga, the wood-burning Ben Loder, named after an Erie railroad magnate and which became a tow boat, once dragging 70 barges in its wake before flames ended its career; the John Arnot, which also burned; the triple-decked P. H. Field, renamed the Onondaga, which in the heyday of Watkins Glen carried as many as 1,000 passengers and which in 1898 was destroyed by dynamite in an elaborately planned spectacle after it had housed a show troupe beset with small pox; the W. W. Langdon, later called the Schuyler; the W. B. Dunning, the D. S. Magee, the Elmira, the Otetiani, renamed the Seneca, which sank at Watkins in 1908; the Colonial and the Watkins.

Now the old docks and landings are rotted away. It has been many a year since a steamboat has touched at Hector Falls, Lodi Landing, Peach Orchard, Dey's Landing, Glenora, Fir Point, Starkey Point or Dresden.

In frontier days busiest of all the ports was Hector Falls on the east shore. It was known then as Factory Falls because around the cascade there clustered flour and woolen mills, a foundry, a potash works and other mills. In 1823, the schooner Mary and Hannah, out of Hector Falls, made navigation history when it slid into the port of New York with a cargo of wheat, butter and beans, first vessel to pass through the completed eastern portion of the Erie Canal via Seneca Lake and river and a private lock at Waterloo.

It was in Hector that the word, "teetotaler" is said to have originated. In 1818 the local temperance society was split into two factions. One wanted a total abstinence pledge to include beer and wines. The other aimed only at curbing the drinking of distilled spirits. When the vote was recorded, the teller placed a "T" before the names of those who signed the total abstinence ballot and they were called "T-Totalers."

Travelers on the road along the eastern shore hear a sound of rushing waters near Hector and there, almost splashing into the highway, is a picturesque waterfall. You'll find them all around Seneca Lake.

North of Hector is the hamlet known as Valois, earlier North Hector. Valois Castle is gone from under the hill. Years ago an international lawyer of that name chose the scenic spot for his Summer home, and remodeled a farm house into a mansion. He imported rare furniture from France, including a bed in which the Empress Eugenie was supposed to have slept. Valois drilled for salt on his land and obtained enough gas to light his castle—but no salt. The mansion later became an inn and finally went up in flames.

As in the time of Sullivan's raid, the eastern shore still is fruit country, especially in the southern reaches, where peaches, cherries, grapes and apples form a considerable crop.

Always rivals have been the neighboring villages with the classical names of Lodi and Ovid. Near Lodi Landing the lake reaches its greatest depth. Because Silver Thread Falls, a 160-foot pillar of water, is off the main road, tourists miss a scenic highlight of the region. The falls are hidden away under the Lehigh Valley tracks near Lodi station and to find them in their rock-walled canyon requires a walk along the tracks and then down a steep path.

Travelers remember Ovid because of the curious "Three Sisters" on the hill at the turn of the road, the old red brick buildings that are court house, library and jail, all in a row and of three sizes like the "Three Bears" of the nursery tale. Seneca is one of 24 double-shire counties in the nation. Her courts have been held alternately at Ovid and Waterloo for more than a century. Ovid was chosen as the first county seat in 1804 and the first court was convened in a barn. The village, lying between Cayuga and Seneca Lakes and founded in 1788, was an important crossroads in the days of the fluctuating frontier.

The Civil War and the capture of the state land grant funds by Cornell ended a dream of the backers of the state's first College of Agriculture which had been opened—briefly —in 1860 on Seneca Lake near Ovid. Instead of a college on the site, they got a state asylum for the insane. It's still there. Willard State Hospital was named after the physician who dramatically fell dead while making a plea for adequate care of the mentally ill before a legislative committee in Albany.

Glenora once was a lively port on the west shore near the head of the lake. Rock Stream provides a natural background

Cavern Cascade in Watkins Glen

Hobart's Mellow Old Campus

of gorge, glen and waterfall for today's pleasant Summer colony, which includes Elmira and Corning people.

To the north is Lakemont, the site of Lakemont Academy which began life in 1842 as Starkey Seminary and was re-opened in 1939 as a college preparatory school for boys. Near Starkey was the first colony of the followers of the fantastic Jemima Wilkinson, "The Universal Friend," whose story will be told in a later chapter. That settlement in 1788 was the first west of Seneca Lake.

Under old trees in Dresden village stands a 152-year-old house, vacant and boarded up. There's a historical marker in front of it. In that house in 1833 Robert G. Ingersoll was born, a minister's son who became the foremost agnostic of his time. He also became a Civil War hero, a silver tongued politico-lawyer and the most controversial figure of the post Civil War period. His name is still anathema in the Bible Belts of America.

A big Dupont plant which manufactures chemicals used by the Navy and a power plant have in recent years quick-ened the tempo of life in Dresden village.

And there is—or was—Kendaia on the eastern shore, the "Appletown" of the Senecas. Sullivan's troops found it a village of 20 log houses, surrounded by corn fields which they burned. They found it ringed with apple trees full of ripening fruit which they cut down. It must have given the thrifty New Englanders in the ranks many a twinge to de-stroy so much "property." Sullivan's men also found the showy, painted tombs of the ancestors of the tribe. These they left alone.

White settlers built a community on the site—a couple of

89

stores, a church, a cemetery, a huddle of houses. It was just a little place that tourists whizzed by and hardly noticed— before Pearl Harbor.

They notice that landscape today. For 15 miles along the lake stretches the Seneca Ordnance Depot and the rejuvenated "city" of Sampson. At Kendaia is a 9,600-acre reservation of concrete igloos and powder storehouses surrounded by 20 miles of wire.

When the War Department took over that tract in 1941, it meant that 100 families had to move. They were paid for their lands, in most cases liberally. They were given a chance to harvest their crops. But nevertheless it was sad business for many whose ancestors were among the first settlers along that shore.

A year later when the 2,700-acre, half million dollar Sampson Naval Station project was launched, the story was the same. Only more cottagers had to leave their Summer havens. The lake shore from Kendaia past Pontius Point, the trout fishermen's paradise, on to Bartlett Beach went into the maw of the World War 2 naval station that was named after the Spanish War admiral who was born in Palmyra.

Sampson bloomed and faded and now it is in full bloom again. Again war is striking the Seneca shore with tremendous impact. That shore has known so many eras—Senecas, settlers, steamboats, slumber, Sampson, somnolence and again Sampson.

The white man has kept shifting the scenes along the lake that "has no bottom, that never freezes," whose Indian name means "place of the stone."

But he has never curbed the willful, hoydenish spirit of

the lake itself. He has not hushed the murmur of the falling waters on the rocky shores. He has not kept back the stormy waves from dashing over old Seneca's foot, to peril the traffic on the white man's motor road.

And he has never stilled the rumble of the guns, the beat of the drums beneath the waters, sounding the last roll call for the Keepers of the Western Door.

Chapter 7

Watkins Wonderland

The pioneers who cleared the land at the head of Seneca Lake some 150 years ago were practical men.

They regarded Watkins Glen gorge as so much worthless land, just a mess of rock where no crop could ever grow.

Today that "worthless land" is a state park, whose scenic grandeur has spread the fame of Watkins Glen all over the world. Through nearly a century thousands of beauty lovers have beaten a path to the natural wonderland of waterfalls, gorges, glens, grottoes and caverns that is Watkins Glen.

It was a newspaper man engaged in that immemorial side line of his craft, press agenting, who first publicized its scenic glories. But that's getting ahead of the story.

Watkins Glen is not only the name of a park. It also is the name of a historic village, a trading center, once a famous health resort and the site of an important salt industry. But its principal industry is the tourist trade.

In 1779 Sullivan's army, flushed with victory over the Senecas and their Tory allies at Newtown (Elmira) passed through the site on their swing around the lakes to lay waste the Indian domain.

There was an isolated white settler or two as early as 1788. In 1794 a syndicate headed by John W. Watkins and Royal Flint bought 325,000 acres of land and founded a settlement at the head of Seneca Lake. The real father of the village was English-born Dr. Samuel Watkins, brother of the proprietor, who took over 2,500 acres including the site of the Glen.

He was struck by the beauty of the place which he called Salubria and by the water power of Glen Creek rushing down through the gorge. At the present entrance of the state park he built grist and saw mills and dug a flume through the cliff at Sentry Bridge. It still can be seen.

Doctor Watkins believed in the village's commercial future because of its position on the lake and he laid out broad parallel streets after a metropolitan plan.

When in 1827 the Chemung Canal was dug to connect the Chemung River at Elmira with Seneca Lake at Watkins, Sam Watkins' dream of a metropolis seemed about to be fulfilled. Watkins built the Jefferson Hotel in 1834. It still stands in the heart of the village. The community was incorporated as Jefferson in 1842. But the canal boom was short-lived and the lakeside village, renamed Watkins in 1852, adding "Glen" in 1926, languished—until it capitalized on its scenic assets.

Watkins Glen is the seat of Schuyler, one of the youngest and smallest of Upstate counties. But it was not always the shire town. When Schuyler was created in 1854, Havana, now Montour Falls, was chosen as the county seat. For 14 years there ensued one of those county seat wars so common in the early days. The board of supervisors refused to take possession of the new county buildings at Havana and held court instead in rented quarters at Watkins three miles to the northward. The rival villages carried their feud into the courts. In 1868 Watkins triumphed and the seat of government has been there ever since.

In the midst of the county seat strife, J. Morvalden Ellis, a newspaper man from Norwalk, Conn., arrived to carry the Watkins banner in the press. He wrote reams of copy about the superior advantages of Watkins as the shire town and he fell in love with the Glen. He was the first to see its commercial resort potentialities and in 1863 he raised some capital and built some rude paths and benches, opening the spot to the tourist trade.

Ellis continued to write glowing newspaper articles about the Glen's beauty and the first year he saw 8,000 to 10,000 visitors come to Watkins. They paid an admission fee. Morvalden Ellis, the scribe with the white beard and his crippled foot in an iron shoe, was the father of the Glen.

It was Ellis who named most of the picturesque spots in the Glen. Some of those apt names are Rainbow Falls, Frowning Cliff, Shadow Gorge, Pillars of Beauty, Artist's Dream, Pulpit Rock, Glen Cathedral, Elfin Gorge, Cavern Cascade, Lover's Ramble, Fairy Pool, Diamond Falls, Glen of the Pools.

Private operators succeeded Ellis. One of them gained wide publicity for the resort by sending railroad tickets to every editor and his wife in the East. Health resorts and hotels were built and lake boats and excursion trains brought thousands of seekers after beauty and health.

In 1906 the park was acquired by the American Scenic and Historical Preservation Society. In 1911 the Glen came under control of the State Park Commission. Since then it has been greatly improved and many stairways and bridges built, some of them 160 feet above the racing waters. Anyone who tours the entire Glen on foot knows he has had a hike, a lot of it uphill. But the beauty he has seen more than compensates for his aching feet.

The Glen has seen some throngs in its long history but nothing like the 350,000 people who invaded the park the Labor Day weekend of 1934. They came to see a strange and heart-gripping spectacle, a deer, stranded on a narrow ledge on the side of a sheer cliff. A local newswriter, Arthur Richards, sent out the story and wire services fed it to papers all over the country.

For three days all sorts of strategems were used to lure the deer to safety but in vain. An Indian tried his woodland lore. A special bridge was built and hoisting apparatus brought in. Finally on September 8, three men worked the deer down the cliff and into a stream whence the graceful, frightened creature, unharmed, bounded down 123 stone steps to freedom.

Down through the beautiful Glen that had brought fame and fortune to the lakeside village, death and destruction rode on the crest of the flood waters of Glen Creek on a July night in 1935. A record cloudburst had swollen the little mountain streams to bursting and the angry waters, assembling in the hills, joined forces to charge through the Glen and attack the low-lying village.

A school teacher lost her life when her home was swept away, 175 families were made temporarily homeless, damage in the region was in the millions. The same flood struck Ithaca and Hornell. The contours of the state park at Watkins were altered by the flood waters. State troopers stood guard, tourists were marooned and isolated from home and kin until communications were restored. The village water was contaminated and drinking water trucked in from Geneva and Horseheads. It was a week before normalcy was restored to Watkins Glen.

Only the comfortable old Jefferson is left of all the hotels that once vied for the tourist trade in the horse and buggy days when the railroad station and the docks swarmed with hacks.

The old Glen Mountain House, for years a tourist rendezvous on the south side of the Glen, burned in 1903. Gone is the Glen Park Hotel with its broad lawns and mineral springs, near the park entrance. Once its proprietor bought a village horse trolley line so that he could extend the rails to the doors of his hotel.

The grandest and most famous of them all was the Glen Springs Hotel and Health Resort, perched on a hill 300 feet above the village and commanding a 20-mile view of lake and hills. In its heyday it made Watkins Glen a spa that was a little Saratoga.

The astute William E. Leffingwell bought the then Lakeview House in 1890, after analysis of the Deer Lick Springs on the property showed the mineral waters to be five times as strong as those of Bad Nauheim's in Germany. To the three-story hotel with wings and cottages after the Saratoga pattern, came some of the nation's elite, among them John D. Rockefeller, Sr., General Pershing, Vice President Curtis, Prince Otto of Austria, actresses, magnates, literary lights. A herd of pure bred Guernsey cattle ranged the 100-acre farm and the links swarmed with golfers.

The Glen Springs, on its hilltop, escaped the flood but it was engulfed by the great depression. It closed its doors during World War 2. The rich furnishings, silver and linen were sold and scattered over the countryside. Some of it found its way into dining cars and rooming houses. In 1946 the old hotel provided emergency housing for GI students of Cornell University and their families. Since 1949 it has been Padua High School and St. Anthony Minor Seminary operated by Franciscan Friars.

After the Sullivan invasion, the Senecas stole back to the Catharine marsh, south of Watkins, seeking, like the wild deer, the salt deposited there for centuries. In later days the Indians would borrow kettles of the pioneers and return them filled with brine. But it was not until 1892 that the salt industry was developed at the head of Seneca Lake. That year the Glen Salt Company, now a part of the International, drilled a well on the west shore. In 1896 the Watkins Salt Company began operations at the southern tip of the lake. The salt is extracted through the evaporation process.

In mid September for the past four years the main street of Watkins Glen and the steep and curving roads around the Glen have become a speedway. The village is the scene of the American Grand Prix, copied after the famous auto road races of Europe. It brings to a village of 3,000 the cream of the nation's amateur racers and sometimes as many as 75,000 spectators.

There are only two miles of straightaway in the course's 6.6 mile circle of dizzy curves and steep grades. The race starts in the village's Main Street where bales of hay are packed around the sides of buildings, hydrants and poles—

just in case. There have been several crackups but only one fatality in the Grand Prix so far. On the straightaway a top speed of 100 miles an hour has been recorded. Seventy miles per hour is average. The course includes a dirt road over the tracks of the New York Central which holds up its trains during the race. There are other thrills besides those of its scenery in Watkins Glen in mid-September.

A remarkable citizen is Frank W. Severne, editor of the Watkins Glen Express. He is at 93 a successful publisher, a political "elder statesman" in Schuyler County, an orator, a poet and philosopher and an expert checker player. He travels about the streets of his village, unaided save at the crossings. You don't think that's so remarkable? But Frank Severne has been blind since the age of 11!

* * *

Three miles south of Watkins Glen along the salt-laden Catharine marsh and the lake inlet stands French Catharine's town of song and story, the old village now called Montour Falls, where cascading waters almost spill into the principal street.

A hub of seven glens and waterfalls, its hills are full of beauty, not so spectacular or so well publicized as those of its old rival, Watkins Glen.

Over 170 years have gone by since Sullivan's troopers put the torch to the log "palace" of Queen Catharine Montour, since they leveled the Indian village. Twice since then the name of the town has been changed but still somehow the spirit of that long dead, half breed sovereign seems to hover over the scene. Her name is perpetuated in the Catharine marsh and the Catharine Creek, as well as in the present name of the village. In the village there's a "Catharine Spring." People down that way pronounce it "Cathar-een," accenting and dragging out the last syllable.

Catharine Montour was a woman of grace and intelligence. Strange mixed blood ran in her veins. Her great grandfather was a French immigrant to Canada who married a Huron wife. Her grandmother was the famous Madame Montour who as a girl was adopted by Frontenac, the French governor of Canada and whose husband was an Oneida chief. Her mother was "French Margaret" wife of a Mohawk. Her sister was "Queen Esther," also known as "The Fiend of Wyoming" because she wielded tomahawk and fire brand as earnestly as any of her warriors at the massacre of the Pennsylvania settlers.

French Catharine married Thomas Hudson, a Seneca chief. They lived in Pennsylvania on the banks of the Tioga until his death. Then his widow stayed for a time at Canisteo Castle before she came to rule over the place the whites called French Catharine's Town although to the Indians it was Shequaga.

It was to Catharine's Town that the broken remnants of the Seneca-Tory army fled after their defeat near Elmira. The queen wanted to make a stand but her advisers counseled flight. She fled to Fort Niagara and after the war lived in Canada. There is a tradition in Montour Falls that she is buried near the site of her old palace.

Montour Falls, first named Havana, was settled in 1788. When the Chemung Canal was built, it became an important port as the head of navigation on the Seneca Lake inlet.

About the village there persists an air of consequence. The town hall with its stately dome beside the Shequaga Falls is a reminder of the county seat war that Havana lost. Beside it, the former jail and another old county office are now private residences.

The town owed much of its early prestige to Charles Cook. He built the massive Montour House, which still stands after 100 years, although it is no longer an inn. As a state senator Cook pushed through the creation of Schuyler County over the agonized protests of three other counties from which it was carved. And he fought hard to keep the county seat at Havana. A bachelor, he built St. Paul's Episcopal Church as a memorial to a girlhood sweetheart who died. He engaged a French artisan to fresco the interior in Old World style.

His crowning achievement was the People's College. In 1860 he conceived the idea of a school which would combine book learning with practical and related work. On the southern outskirts of the village a square, plain and sturdy six-story building arose, from bricks made in a nearby field. Lack of funds caused the People's College to lose the state land grant fund to Ezra Cornell's new university at Ithaca although Charles Cook made a valiant fight for his dream college.

In 1872 Elbert Cook, brother of the senator, established Cook Academy on the campus of the People's College. A preparatory school for boys, it lasted until the second World War when it closed its doors. From its ivy-covered walls went out many famous graduates, among them Wellington Koo, the Chinese statesman. The old Cook Academy now is

St. John's Atonement Seminary which trains missionary friars of the Franciscan Atonement order.

A native son, even more politically powerful than Charles Cook, was David Bennett Hill, who moved to Elmira and became governor of the state, a United States Senator and a power in the national Democracy. The bald head and the drooping mustache of the "Sage of Wolfert's Roost" were familiar to newspaper readers for decades. Hill died in 1910 and is buried near the scenes of his boyhood.

Montour Falls (it changed its name from Havana in 1890) never rivaled Watkins Glen as a health or summer resort. But for 35 years after 1878 the water cure and magnesia spring of Bethsada were widely patronized.

Among the many glens in the rugged hills, Montour Glen is outstanding. Waters descend 400 feet through one and one quarter miles of rocky canyon, in alternating rapids, falls and pools, finally to spill over a 156-foot cliff, at the head of the village's principal street. Louis Philippe, the royal French exile, once sketched those Shequaga Falls, "tumbling waters" in the Indian language. His handiwork hangs in the Louvre today. And long ago Red Jacket, the Seneca Demosthenes, inflamed with white man's firewater, pitted his mighty voice against the thunder of the tumbling waters.

In the early Spring the waters of the Catharine Creek present a thrilling spectacle. It is the annual run of the lake trout from the hills into Seneca Lake. Hundreds of beauties, some of them king size, leap in the foaming waters. When the season opens, the banks of the Catharine and other streams are literally lined with fishermen. They swarm Havana Glen and Deckertown Falls. They far outnumber the fish in the streams. And often by the time the season opens, most of the big fellows are out in the inland lake. They say they bite best when the lilacs are in bloom.

Chapter 8

Geneva, "The Beleaguered City"

"The old order changeth, yielding place to new."

Stately old Geneva, at the foot of Seneca Lake, clung to the old order a long, long time.

But even that citadel of traditions, with its colleges, its Trinity Church and the mansions of its "Quality Folk" on its elm-bordered Hill, and its factories, business district, railroad tracks and the rest of its people on its undistinguished Flats, has been yielding to the onslaughts of the new order.

Two wartime mass invasions in the last decade have had a lot to do with that. When a city of 45,000 Bluejackets springs up at the doors of a city of 17,000, the smaller city is bound to feel the impact—as Geneva did during World War 2 when Sampson, the second largest naval training center in America, flowered 14 miles away. And now after a short "armistice," the invasion is on again. This time it is from the same Sampson, now an Air Force training base with an eventual population of 34,000. It housed 20,000 trainees when this was written.

So Geneva, like the old gray mare, "ain't what she used to be." But she still is a distinctive, lively and altogether attractive city.

But two wars, a desperate housing shortage, the decimation wrought by death and taxes among the Old Families

103

who lived in the pillared, wistaria-clad mansions have raised hob with old traditions.

The patrician tradition goes back a long way. When York State was a province of the British Crown, Kanadesaga, on the site of Geneva, was a place of consequence in the domain of the Senecas, the residence of their hereditary king.

The British realized Kanadesaga's strategic position and in 1756 Sir William Johnson caused a stockade of pine and oak to be built there. The Tory Walter Butler had his barracks, storehouse and residence in the town and from Kanadesaga he and the old king, Sauquanquethagtha, led their hordes of painted Senecas and Tory renegades to the massacre of the settlers in the Wyoming Valley.

The village of 50 well built homes amid fields and orchards was near the present State Agricultural Experiment Station. Sullivan's men wiped it off the face of the landscape.

Geneva was the first white settlement in Western New York except for the Jemima Wilkinson colony. As early as 1788 Lark Jennings was living in a log cabin along Seneca Lake at the foot of the present Washington Street and near the old sulphur spring.

In early days a group of land speculators, including Hudson River gentry, launched a bold scheme to grab a vast tract. The law forbade purchase of land from Indians by individuals. So the land syndicate sought a 999-year lease by treaty. The group hatched a secession plot to create a separate state, even maintaining an armed force, until the courts, the Federal Government and Governor George Clinton combined to foil the "Long Lease" conspiracy. Geneva was the headquarters of the "Long Lease" outfit. By 1790 there were a dozen families in the settlement.

When the New England promoters, Phelps and Gorham, purchased two million acres of wilderness, Geneva was picked as the center of the enterprise. But a survey indicated the place was outside the purchase. So Phelps shifted his land office to Canandaigua. The first survey of the Pre-emption Line, so called because it defined the limits of Massachusetts' pre-emptive rights, was shown to have been faulty, either by error or design. The new line brought Geneva within the purchase.

Part of the Phelps and Gorham holdings passed into the hands of a British syndicate headed by Sir William Pulteney. This sale brought to the Lakes Country one of the most arresting figures of a colorful period, Charles Williamson, the land agent for the Pulteney syndicate. This courtly Scottish-born former British officer, a man of vast energy and vision, played an important part in the development of early Geneva.

Williamson is credited with having named the city because he was struck by its resemblance to the Old World Geneva beside another sparkling lake. Historians have discovered that the place was called Geneva before the land agent laid eyes on it.

Geneva had a key place in the Williamson colonization blueprint. He planned a settlement on the wooded plateau overlooking the lake. There he laid out the broad Main Street and the public square after the English pattern. Pulteney Square is still there under its old trees. Williamson built on that square in 1794 the finest hotel in the frontier.

To that "Astor House of the West," he brought from London as its landlord the famous Thomas Powell of the Thatched Cottage. A grand ball heralded the opening of the hotel and attracted a strange assemblage—Southern aristocrats lured to the new land through Williamson's promotions, Senecas, land promoters, adventurers, backwoodsmen, hunters, trappers.

Williamson laid out terraced gardens extending from his hotel down the slopes to the lake. He set out shade trees. He forbade any building across the street that would obstruct the view of the lake. It was only after he lost his land agent position that there arose opposite the Square and along South Main Street the quaint row of houses, with their backs to the lake, reminiscent of towns in the Hudson Valley and the South, that today gives the street such a distinctive air.

The land agent built a mansion at Mile Point up the lake. He launched the first boat on Seneca. Geneva became a popular stopping place on the road across the state. It was a gateway to the frontier and stage coaches and settlers' wagons in increasing numbers pulled up before the splendid Williamson Hotel on the Square.

It was through the promotions of Charles Williamson that the Southerners came to the Lakes Country, to found in Geneva an enduring tradition of spacious living. He induced the Maryland Fitzhughs to buy land in the Genesee Country and although they established their estates elsewhere, for a time they lived in Geneva and sent word back to the South of the richness of the frontier.

In 1801 two cavalcades came over the Cumberland Trail. John Nicholas and Robert Rose and their families in their

106

ponderous coaches, with their retinues of Negro slaves and wagons piled high with elegant furnishings, had left their Virginia estates for new homes in the Lakes Country. Nicholas settled at White Springs, until recently the Alfred G. Lewis estate. Rose built across the lake the mansion with the pillars that to this day is known as Rose Hill.

They were gentlemen farmers, cultured, open handed people and they founded the aristocratic tradition in Geneva. In 1827 their slaves were freed by state law but most of them remained with their former masters to work for wages.

Southern planters, retired New York merchants, descendants of Dutch patroons, with a sprinkling of churchmen and professors, gave Geneva a social tone and a way of life that was different than any other community in the region.

In 1818 Elkanah Watson wrote: "Geneva is not only an elegant but a salubrious village and distinguished for its refinement and elevated character of its inhabitants." Elkanah was a widely traveled and discriminating man.

More than a century later a native Genevan, Warren Hunting Smith of the Yale faculty, wrote a little book built around Watson's quotation. He titled it "Geneva, New York—An Elegant and Salubrious Village."

Warren Smith knew whereof he wrote. He was reared in the rarefied atmosphere of the Hill and he painted an intriguing picture of the South Main Street that used to be.

In the high ceilinged rooms of the mansions on the Hill, behind the white pillars, lived gentlefolk of good taste and good manners, who had fine linen, old family silver and china, who collected rare books and paintings, who wrote little volumes of poetry which they published at their own

107

expense and did a little painting, mostly for their own amusement, who traveled much and were never noisy or ostentatious.

Their men knew the correct way to carry a stick. Their ladies languidly sketched the scenic beauties of the lake. They rode in carriages behind good horses, driven by well trained coachmen. They entertained distinguished guests. They were of the leisure class. They lived mostly on inherited wealth. None of them was enormously wealthy. Some of them were downright poor. But money did not count. Birth was all that mattered. Newly rich tradesmen who tried to crash the gates of The Hill retreated before a wall of stony indifference.

Here was no land-holding, fox hunting dynasty as in the Genesee Valley. Here was only a gracious way of life. Little old spinster sisters, like the fictitious "Misses Elliott" of Warren Smith's later book, even after their resources shrank to the vanishing point, still held their heads high as they minced down South Main Street, in all their shabby gentility. They still belonged.

They married within their own circle until nearly everybody on the Hill were cousins. And always there were Hobart College and Trinity Church to give the proper cultural touch. The social orbit revolved about the church whose Gothic tower has survived fire and the years to dominate the South Main Street scene. It was fashionable for the elite to teach the Negro children in Trinity's Sunday-school. Anyone could teach white children.

Fortunes might melt away, the old mansions might pass

into alien hands. Eccentricities were forgiven if the eccentric one belonged. And belonging was a matter of birth.

Such was the way of life in one part of Geneva, whose elegance remained undimmed until the new century came. With it came snorting, smelly automobiles, country clubs, jazz, a new pushing smartness, get rich quick interlopers—and the old order yielded inch by inch. Many of the Old Families died off—without issue.

Then came the wars and Sampson and now only the remnants of the old regime are left to guard the Hill.

It must be remembered that the Hill was—and is—only one part of Geneva.

Williamson planned the commercial center on the plateau above the lake. That plan was not fulfilled. Trade and industry stayed on the bottoms although a railroad dared to edge its way along the lake shore, hidden under the brow of the sacred Hill.

The city grew and prospered. It was set in a rich farming country and Geneva became its center. Steamboats, railroads, industries came until more and more smoke rolled out over Seneca water. Nurseries flourished on the borders of the town—and still do.

The Irish came early, to dig the canals and build the railroads. They stayed to go into trade and definitely into politics. The Old Families never controlled the political destinies of Geneva. Maybe they never wanted to. At any rate in traditionally Republican Ontario County, wards along the railroad tracks in Geneva sometimes upset the apple cart.

Today Geneva has a sizeable Italian population and a picturesque Syrian colony. There must always be hewers of wood and drawers of water, even in "an elegant and salubrious" village.

* * *

Geneva has been a college town since 1822. Hobart is one of the oldest colleges in the state. It also is one of the smallest and is far from being the wealthiest.

Episcopal Bishop John Henry Hobart established it as Geneva College and picked its site above Seneca's waters. It was a union of Fairfield Theological School and Geneva Academy, the latter established in 1796. Through a grant from Trinity Church in New York, conditioned on the establishment of a branch divinity school, two buildings went up on the hill. Geneva Hall and Trinity Hall are still there. There is dignity in their time-worn stones.

Despite its ecclesiastical origin, Hobart's charter contained a guarantee of absolute religious freedom to all members, regardless of denomination. It pioneered in introducing an "English course" to supplement the traditional "classical" course. This forerunner of the modern scientific curriculum was designed to "train farmers, mechanics, manufacturers and merchants in direct reference to the practical business of life." Years later Ezra Cornell had the same idea.

From 1834 to 1872 when it was moved to Syracuse, the Medical College was part of Geneva College, renamed Hobart in 1851. The old medical school burned in 1870 and there's a marker at the site because it is historic.

In 1847 the dean of that school looked over a roomful of young men students and, with a quizzical look in his eye, said:

"Gentlemen, I have here the application of one Elizabeth Blackwell of Philadelphia for admission to this college as a student. I am submitting it for your approval. What is your decision?"

The students received the announcement with howls of laughter. Of course it was a hoax inspired by some rival school. The dean's expression told them that he, too, regarded it as a joke. A woman studying medicine? A woman rolling pills, taking pulses and delivering babies? It was preposterous, it was unthinkable—in 1847.

So the young men voted with a whoop to accept the application and proceeded to draft a long-winded, facetious resolution in reply which stated their conviction that "a pretty girl should do much to make medicine interesting."

A few weeks later to their stupefied amazement, a slim, serious girl of 26, demure in dark clothes, not pretty but self possessed and gracious, presented herself at the office of the dean. Elizabeth Blackwell had come to Geneva Medical College. A dream had come true for this British-born former school teacher who had met with many rebuffs in her long campaign to gain entrance to a medical school.

During her two years at Geneva, it is recorded that she conducted herself with "propriety and discretion." Her position was a difficult one, a lone girl among scores of men. She was barred from delicate surgical operations. When she was present, frankness evaporated from classroom discussions. Geneva society ostracized her. Professional careers, especially the practice of medicine, were not the thing for young ladies.

Nevertheless in 1849 Elizabeth Blackwell, her eyes clouded

111

with happy tears, clutched a hard won roll of parchment, the first medical diploma ever granted to a woman in America.

Little Hobart has weathered the shock of three major wars and many a financial crisis. The old college has a generous, tolerant spirit, and she never sought to mold her students into any narrow, rigid pattern. She always has regarded the exuberance and follies of youth with kindly understanding. Even in the early days, the sons of wealthy churchmen were inclined to pranks. In recent years the collegians have delighted in draping with the proper garments the nude female figure that stands in Pulteney Square as a World War I memorial.

Hobart is democratic. Her doors have been opened to many a farm lad from Oaks Corners and Benton Center, to sons of Irish Catholic cops as well as sons of Episcopal dignitaries.

In 1906 William Smith, wealthy, woman-hating, bachelor nurseryman, gave half a million dollars to found a woman's college whose courses would co-ordinate with Hobart's. The present William Smith College on the hill north of the Hobart campus is the result. Officially the two schools are the Colleges of the Seneca. Nobody ever calls them that in ordinary conversation.

*   *   *

Geneva is full of landmarks. On the Hill there is 110-year-old Trinity Church, birthplace of the Western New York Episcopal Church in 1838. More than a decade ago flames damaged the edifice, which has been rebuilt to conform wherever possible to the original design, copied from Trinity in New York City. Once the Geneva church had a quartet composed of Mrs. Bear, Mrs. Partridge, Mr. Fox and Mr. Fowle.

Pulteney Square is redolent of history. The apartment house there is on the site of the pioneer Williamson Hotel. Later on it was the Hygienic Institute, a health resort which piped its mineral waters from the old spring at the foot of steep Washington Street. Once the water was bottled and shipped away. A stock company was formed. It issued handsome certificates but the venture was unprofitable.

When the present Genesee Park, under its shade trees and flanked by old residences, was given to the city, the deed provided that it should always carry the name of Franklin Park, the fence must ever be maintained and no buildings permitted there. Every one of the provisions has been violated.

A venerable landmark is the Lafayette Tree. In 1825 when Lafayette visited Geneva, he rested under its spreading branches. Nearby is the former Maple Hill mansion, now the Lafayette Inn. Its stables, in which stands the carriage in which Lafayette rode, are called the "Priory" and once they housed the strangest school in America.

It existed in the fancy of its eccentric owner, the late Charles D. Bean. He called it "Endymion Military Preparatory School." He sent out catalogs, picturing the swimming pool and the churchly nave. The swimming pool was only 18 inches deep and served far better as a cock pit than a swimming pool. Bean had some beautifully embossed diplomas printed. One of them, it was said, gained for a Genevan entrance into a midwest college. There were class mottoes on the walls. There were all the accoutrements of a school—but there never was a student.

Bean was an attorney, a world traveler, an authority on early American history and on lore of the Free Masons. Once he owned the desk of William Morgan, foe of Free Masonry whose disappearance plunged the land into political turmoil.

On one of his trips abroad, Bean met Sarah Bernhardt and on his farm near Prattsburg, he erected a curious memorial to the divine Sarah. The memorial, a pillar of concrete blocks, about six feet square and eight feet tall, has this inscription in bold letters:

"To Madame Sarah Bernhardt, the Greatest Actress on Earth whose Lyric Fire and Divine Voice gave more Intense and Supreme Life to the Poets; in profound admiration is built this rugged memorial by the Knights of Cypress and Devoted Friends."

Who were the Knights of Cypress? Only Charley Bean knew.

There is another odd memorial near Geneva. It is on the lake road about nine miles north of Sampson. The six-foot-high metal statue is dedicated to "Fido, Our Faithful Friend, died May 16, 1913, aged 13 years, 9 months." On the base is the name, "Zobrist," and atop the memorial is the figure of a toy bulldog. An anchor is carved on one side and an open book, possibly a Bible, on another. It is said the statue disappears sometimes on Hallowe'en nights and is recovered miles away.

Nearby in the Town of Fayette a historical marker points out the farm where John Johnston in 1835 installed the first tile drains ever used in America. He sent to England for them.

At Castle and North Streets in Geneva is one of the few octagonal houses left in the region to remind us of a fad of a century ago.

In the rear of the brick house at 620 Castle Street stands the red-domed observatory in which the benign, bearded Dr. William R. Brooks of the Hobart faculty (the students called him "Sky" Brooks) studied the heavens. He discovered more comets, 27 of them, than any other American astronomer of his time.

Another Genevan, probably the best known on the national scene, was Charles J. Folger, who lived in one of the South Main Street mansions and who was secretary of the treasury under President Arthur.

On Castle Street hill at the junction with North Main is a stone boulder, Geneva's tribute to Policeman Aeneas McDonald, who in 1924 was slain by a bandit he was trying to capture. The killing of a popular police officer stirred the city deeply. Hence the memorial at a busy intersection.

Near the site of the Indian village of Kanadesaga on the northeastern edge of the city, science since 1862 has been waging a quiet yet effective battle for the farmers of the state. There, at the State Agricultural Experiment Station, an affiliate of Cornell University, hundreds of methods of improving crops, fruit and dairy products and of eliminating pests and disease have been evolved.

The station is in a productive countryside. For more than a century Geneva has been a nursery center. Once there were 50 nurseries on her outskirts, growing and shipping shrubs, fruit trees and berry bushes all over the land. The nursery industry still is an important one.

Geneva also manufactures a diversity of products, including cereals, optical goods, stoves, forgings. The smoke of industry is concentrated along the lake front and on the Flats, away from the citadel of culture and elegance on the Hill.

Despite an air of subdued gentility, Geneva has long been one of the sportiest cities in the state. Memories are still green of her old race track on the eastern edge of town. The town has always liked prize fights and cock fights and games of chance. She has produced some rather important figures in the gambling fraternity.

The city has loyally supported Hobart's teams. Hundreds of Genevans used to invade Rochester for the big game between Hobart and the UR's gridiron warriors. Three years ago athletic relations were broken off. It seems the Hobart rooters were too vociferous. They hooted during a long and dull plaque ceremony between halves. The then UR prexy was so affronted that he severed the gridiron rivalry of half a century.

Hobart never had a more loyal rooter than Art Kenney, "the mayor of South Exchange Street." In his shoe-shine emporium at Geneva's busiest corner hangs the citation presented him by the Hobart Alumni Council in 1947 as "Christian gentleman, exemplary citizen, a Hobart tradition in his own right." Other testimonials to Art include one signed by a mayor and a fire chief for "outstanding bravery at a fire although not a member of the fire department" and one from the Barber Shop singers' group for "training, experience and support."

In her lifetime Cleo Cameron never received any framed testimonials and there is no marker at the site of her celebrated "business establishment" in Bradford Street along the lake. In its time Cleo's was as famous in this part of the state as Red Dwyer's Bellhurst night club has in another form of entertainment in recent years.

Despite its facade of dignity and elegance, Geneva at heart has always been warm-blooded and never dull.

*   *   *

But the old city, pretty set in its ways, was unprepared for the human avalanche which descended upon it in 1941 when Uncle Sam began building the Seneca Ordnance Depot and Sampson Naval Training Station on the lake.

Workmen poured in from all over the country and there was no place to house them. They slept in the Armory, the City Hall, in parks, trailers and autos.

Then after the station was built, a blue tide surged into Geneva every night. The city virtually became a roaring Navy camp and the blare of the juke boxes in the 20 night spots all but drowned out the thunder of the organ of Trinity Church and the voices of the traditional past. Some of the Old Guard looked a bit askance at the transformation of their once tranquil streets but generally Geneva was hospitable to the sailor boys and equipped a large USO center for them. During World War 2 Sampson brought considerable prosperity to Geneva, along with a new life and color.

The war-born housing shortage, which has never been conquered, brought changes on the Hill. Mansions were remodeled into apartments and temporary wooden barracks mingled incongruously with the old stone and brick buildings on Hobart's serene and mellow campus.

The city had scarcely recovered from the shock of the first Sampson invasion when the Korean war caused reactivation of the former Naval base under the Air Force flag. The place had not long been idle. After World War 2 it was used as a Naval hospital and for three years it was the Sampson State College for war veterans. At its peak there were 2,300 students, many of them married veterans who lived at the base.

After the college closed, the big drill hall and other buildings became a great granary where wheat was stored for the Credit Commodity Corporation. The sprawling former camp lay at the mercy of vandals and thieves and many of the buildings were in sorry shape when in 1950, after Sampson was headed for a future career as a state park, the Army Air Force suddenly took it over as an indoctrination center for its expanding ranks.

The work of rehabilitating Sampson brought scenes reminiscent of 1941, although on a smaller scale. Reconstruction was pushed at breakneck speed because of the congestion at other Air Force bases and workmen, mostly from the area, received some fabulous pay envelopes. A Congressional investigation brought out that one man worked $23\frac{1}{2}$ hours each day for three consecutive days, in addition to 10 hours a day for the balance of the week, and collected a pay check for one week totaling $534.

On February 1, 1951, the Sampson Air Force Base received its first batch of trainees. They have been pouring in and out steadily ever since. Again there is a city larger than Geneva 14 miles away. The housing situation in the whole area again is acute. Geneva is crowded to the eaves, as are Ovid, Waterloo and other nearby communities. For the first time in many a year ferry service is being operated across the lake between Sampson and Dresden twice a day to accommodate Sampson employes who live across Seneca.

One Summer week end there were 3,400 visitors at Sampson. Half of them stayed overnight in Geneva—the Lord knows where. The influx has strained the city's housing facilities to the limit. Considerable building is going on, even out in the White Springs domain of landed gentry. And the manor house at White Springs Farm has become a nursing home.

Air Force trainees during their eight weeks at Sampson have only one day and night of liberty and then must be accompanied by relatives, so the current "invasion" is not so evident on Geneva streets as during the Naval "occupation." However there are 7,000 permanent personnel at the base. Four youths of that personnel, none from the region, staged a recent holdup in Canandaigua and mortally wounded a deputy sheriff in an attempted getaway. But on the whole the record of Sampson, considering its huge and polyglot population, has been a fairly crimeless one.

Geneva is old and when one grows old, it is hard to become used to sweeping changes. But Geneva is a thoroughbred and has faced the challenge with grace and poise. Even the remnants of the Old Guard on the Hill are becoming reconciled to the new order.

Waterloo is an "in-between" village. It lies on Routes 5-20 between Seneca Falls and Geneva and between Lakes Cayuga and Seneca. It is a brisk and individualistic community of more than 4,000 and it falls into no particular orbit, other than it is a part of the Lakes Country.

It is on historic ground. There the Indians had a village of 18 log houses, called Skoyase, "the place of the whortleberries," which, like its neighbors, was destroyed by the ruthless Sullivan in 1779.

The water power of the Seneca River drew the first settlers in 1795. In 1809 the father of the village arrived in the person of Elisha Williams, a lawyer of Hudson, N. Y. who bought a tract along the river and proceeded to develop it. He gave the settlement the name of New Hudson.

Elisha Williams' mansion, built in 1816, now is the village hospital and the names of the Williams clan lives on the village streets—Williams, Elisha, Virginia and Elizabeth. But the village did not keep the name of the old home town of its head man. In 1816, the inhabitants for some reason tired of the name.

At a public meeting a veteran of the Revolution so eloquently urged the name of the battlefield of Napoleon's downfall that the village took the name of Waterloo—and Waterloo it has been ever since.

Since 1817 it has shared honors with Ovid as the shire town of Seneca County. The county buildings border a shady park lined with memorials.

Waterloo's growth was rapid in the second decade of the 19th Century. Flour and grist mills and woolen mills utilized the power of the Seneca River. Some of the big stone and

Keuka Lake in the Vineyard Country

In a Hammondsport Wine Cellar

brick mills built a century ago still stand along the river-canal. The completion of the canal in 1828 boomed the town. The roaring canal days are gone but Waterloo is still a canal town, a port on the link between Cayuga and Seneca Lakes. In later years Waterloo was known as the site of a distillery which made Duffy's Pure Malt Whiskey. The Duffy family has long been prominent in Waterloo and in Rochester.

When the pioneers cleared the land for the Genesee Road in 1795, they found a fine big elm squarely in the projected route. They swerved the highway around the tree and the Patriarch Elm still stands in the village and the busy traffic of Routes 5 and 20 follows the curve there. It is believed to be 350 years old. Its trunk is five feet in circumference. Twenty years ago when disease threatened the landmark, surgeons were engaged to save it. They poured eight tons of cement into the cavity near its base.

Another historic tree grows in Waterloo—or near it. It's two and one half miles west of Waterloo on the road to Geneva and it is known far and wide as the Scythe Tree. From sunup to sundown an American flag waves from it.

In 1861 Wyman Johnson lived with his parents in the farmhouse by the Scythe Tree. The youth heard Lincoln's call to arms and went off to the Civil War. Before he left, he carefully hung his scythe in the crotch of a Balm of Gilead sapling in the yard and said:

"Leave the scythe in the tree until I return."

Wyman Johnson never returned. He died of wounds in a Confederate hospital in Raleigh, N. C. in 1864. But his scythe still hangs in the tree, now 100 feet high and more than five feet thick at its base. The tree is rapidly swallowing the scythe that has made it famous. Less than six inches of blade now protrude from the massive trunk. Long ago the handle rotted away.

In 1917 the war drums beat again and two brothers living on the farm responded to the call as Wyman Johnson had in '61. Before they left for camp, Ray and Lynn Schaffer hung their scythes in the tree in the tradition of the farm. Both returned safely from the war. Each brother took down his scythe from the tree but left the blade. So now there are three scythes in the old tree whose story is part of the folklore of the Lakes Country—and of America.

Two miles south of Waterloo a dirt road leads off Route 96 to one of the Western New York shrines of the Mormon Church. There in a log cabin on the Peter Whitmer farm on April 6, 1830, the Church of Jesus Christ of Latter Day Saints was organized by the "Six Witnesses," Joseph Smith, the prophet-founder; two of his brothers, Oliver Cowdery and David and Joseph Whitmer. From that log cabin in the Town of Fayette Smith directed the missionary work of his followers for more than a year. There the church, born of the visions revealed to Joseph Smith on Cumorah Hill near Palmyra, took tangible form. The "Six Witnesses" have grown to a million and a half "Saints."

The Whitmers went west on the historic Mormon hegira. The farm fell into other hands and the log cabin was torn down in the 1860s. In its place the present large white farmhouse was built. In 1927 the Mormon Church acquired the property as a shrine.

A member of the church, William L. Powell, and his

family, have occupied the place since 1927. They came from Salt Lake City and the farm is operated under direction of headquarters beside the Salt Lake.

The Whitmer Farm has many visitors. During the annual pageant at the sacred hill near Palmyra, two hundred came in one day to see the place where "The Six Witnesses" laid the framework for a mighty church.

Chapter 9

Keuka, "The Lady of the Lakes"

When the great ice blanket was lifted from the land, it left a Y-shaped sheet of water and 70 miles of curving shore-line, dotted with bays and coves, in the Southern York State hills.

The Indians called the shining two-pronged lake Keuka, "canoe landing." The white pioneers called it Crooked Lake. In later years it resumed its older, more picturesque title.

Keuka may lack the wild and mystical grandeur of some of her sisters. She exudes the spirit of peace. She is the lady of the lakes. She is lovely in any season but most enchanting when the first frosts richly tint her vine-clad slopes, when the smoky haze of Autumn hovers over Bluff Point, the promontory that divides the lake into two slender arms.

She is the only Finger Lake of irregular outline. Her waters course from the main inlet at the base of the Y in one of its branches and flow out through a dividing bluff to its outlet at the tip of another fork.

Keuka was the Senecas' fishing paradise just as it later became the white man's. The Indians built no populous villages along it and therefore Sullivan's raiders bypassed it.

But it is rich in historical association. As a boy Red Jacket practiced oratory in the woods around his mother's cabin near Branchport. Above Keuka's waters in the pioneering time Jemima Wilkinson, the Universal Friend, had her fantastic cult. On and around the lake Glenn Hammond Curtiss began the experiments that made him "the father of naval aviation."

And around this lake of the divided waters is one of the greatest vineyard and wine-producing areas in America.

Only pleasure craft ply Keuka today but once it was a pathway of commerce. Like the other lakes it had its colorful era of steamboats and excursion trains.

Early in the 19th Century, an enterprising trader, George McClure of Bath, launched the schooner Sally on the Crooked Lake. It and other vessels transported the settlers' grain and other products to Hammondsport at its southern tip. Thence they were hauled by team the 10 miles to Bath and shipped by raft and ark down the Conhocton to the Susquehanna and the ports of Philadelphia and Baltimore.

The building of the Erie Canal diverted this traffic to northern ports. The outlet of Keuka, the narrow, shallow Minnesetah River, flows into Seneca Lake. But it was inadequate as a commercial channel. So in 1833 the Crooked Lake Canal was dug between Penn Yan at the foot of Keuka Lake to Dresden, seven miles distant, on Seneca Lake. That waterway gave up the ghost in 1870 but the remains of its 28 lift locks and old towpath are still visible. The Fall Brook branch of the New York Central Railroad follows pretty much the old canal bed.

The Steamboat Age dawned in 1837 with the advent of the 80-foot wood-burning Keuka, which was propelled by a central paddle wheel midway between its two hulls. Its principal function was to tow canal boats. It was dismantled after it stranded in the mud in 1848.

Then came the Steuben, a sidewheeler, built in 1845. It burned at its dock in Penn Yan in 1864. Third steamer on the lake was the George R. Young, launched in 1864. Rechristened the Seneca, it was beached in 1879. In 1867 the Keuka, a screw steamer, appeared, followed by the sidewheeler, the Yates, whose 11-year career ended in flames in 1883.

In the 1870s the development of the grape industry brought a new prosperity to the region. Steamboats were needed to haul the grapes and wines and in 1878 a new sidewheeler, the Lulu, made her maiden voyage over the 21 miles of lake. She was fitted out with a former locomotive engine and it was said the roar of her exhaust could be heard 10 miles away.

The Lulu was joined in 1880 by the Urbana, noted for her graceful lines and for the deer painted on her walking beam. She operated until 1904 and figured in the fierce navigation war of the 1880s and '90s.

Around 1882 a Rochester lawyer, William L. Halsey, had a Summer home near Grove Springs on the lake. One day he and his wife were on the Urbana, out of Penn Yan. Because the lake was rough, the skipper refused to land the Halseys at their dock and instead took them to Grove Springs. The lawyer was incensed and told the Urbana captain: "If you can't operate this boat to accommodate the public, I'll build one of my own that will."

It was no idle threat. Halsey interested Rochester and Penn Yan capital in the new Crooked Lake Navigation Company. In 1883 it launched the Farley Holmes, the fastest, largest steamboat the lake had ever seen. Immediately a steamboat war, featured by fare price cutting, began. On its maiden voyage, the Holmes, about to pull into the docks at Penn Yan, found its path blocked by the Urbana, squarely across the channel. The law had to be invoked before the Urbana yielded ground.

The Holmes and the Urbana staged spirited races. The Crooked Lake line did not operate on the Sabbath. The older company did. Both advertised extensively and the fame of Keuka spread. Long excursion trains rumbled into Hammondsport and Penn Yan weekdays as well as week ends. The wine cellars were a popular drawing card. The lake became lined with Summer homes.

In 1887 the Crooked Lake interests built a new boat, faster than the Holmes. It was the William L. Halsey, named after the lawyer who "got even." The line also added the West Branch, a screw steamer, to the fleet, to operate over the western fork of the lake. In 1891 both companies tired of the profitless competition and the Crooked Lake line sold its interests to its rival.

In 1892 the pride of the lake, the all-steel screw steamer, the Mary Bell, which cost $40,000 and had a 600-passenger capacity, made its debut, to reign for 30 years over Keuka's waters. After the Holmes, renamed the Yates, was abandoned in 1915 and the Halsey, which became the Steuben, sank in 1917, there was only the Mary Bell, under a new name, the Penn Yan, left. The West Branch and the little 85-foot Cricket, which had challenged the Mary Bell, had vanished from the scene.

In the Fall of 1922, the Penn Yan nee the Mary Bell, made her last trip with passengers. The rest of that season she carried grapes—22,500,000 pounds were shipped that year from Hammondsport—and then the last of the Keuka Lake steamboats docked for the last time. For years she swung at anchor at Hammondsport, stripped of her machinery and brass, until finally she rotted away and slipped into the lake she once had ruled.

The Steamboat Age evokes memories of the resorts along the lake, of Grove Springs and its big hotel and dancing pavilion, of Ogoyago on the western shore, of Idlewild, of the Ark, of Gibson's Landing, of Tanglewood and Urbana and its ivy-clad stone winery. Steamboats no longer dock at Keuka but the gracious old Hotel Keuka is still there in its picturesque setting of lake and hills. Thousands have danced there through the years and among the college musicians in the orchestras of yesteryear were Fred Waring and Hoagy Carmichael. They weren't big names then.

Seth Green, the greatest angler of his day, paid this tribute to Keuka Lake in 1881 when he was United States fish commissioner:

"I think Lake Keuka unsurpassed by any waters in America as a fishing resort—on Aug. 28 last, I took with hook and line 19 salmon trout, weighing 113 pounds, and on Oct. 1, 1880, 33 black bass weighing 106 pounds."

Green used to make his headquarters at the Keuka Hotel. There he developed the Seth Green rig, 300 feet long, with six leaders to which were attached three treble gang hooks. Game laws were not so strict in those days.

But the wizard of rod and line never caught a fish the way young Harry Morse did nearly 70 years ago.

He was only six years old and his mother had taken him along for company when she went fishing one Summer morning in a little skiff on Brandy Bay near the old distillery.

The lad idly dipped a hand in the water. Then he peered down into the depths that held so much mystery for a six-year old. He bent lower and lower over the side of the boat until his face touched the water.

Intent upon her line, the mother did not notice. Suddenly the boy jerked back his head, screaming. He grabbed frantically at his nose. Something shiny flopped about in the bottom of the boat.

It was a six pound trout and his mother pounced upon it.

Thinking the boy's pink and white proboscis some new and delectable tidbit, the fish had snapped at it and hung on. The sudden pain caused the youngster to throw back his head and pull the big trout into the boat—with his nose.

The story spread and pictures were taken of Harry and the fish he had landed with such unusual bait. Those pictures were put on post cards and sold on the excursion boats on the lake.

When Harry Morse grew up, he became a pilot on one of those lake boats, the Penn Yan. He had a reputation for coolness. Once after he had brought his steamer safely into port during a fierce storm, a Southern poet, Booth Lowery, who was aboard, hearing the confident word passed among the passengers, "It's all right. Harry's at the wheel," wrote a little poem which he titled "Harry's at the Wheel."

After a sojourn on a ranch in the West, Morse returned to Penn Yan where he operated a movie house. He was a shy man and would seldom discuss the piscatorial exploit of his boyhood. To his dying day he carried a scar on his nose to verify the strangest fish story ever told in the Finger Lakes country.

* * *

Like a giant mastiff Bluff Point watches over the waters of the lake it splits into two blue arms. From that headland one can see on a clear day, it is said, seven counties and a dozen lakes. The panorama caught the fancy of aboriginal mound-building tribes who left an embankment there.

Charles Williamson, the land agent, thrilled to its beauty, too. On Bluff Point he built one of his three mansions in the hinterland. Today the historic Wagener manor house is on its peak and the newer Garrett mansion on its slope.

Bluff Point's crowning glory is the exquisite chapel of Gothic stone, a parents' memorial to a beloved son. His name was Charles William Garrett and he was a wine magnate's son. In his 20s, he was stricken with tuberculosis and all Paul Garrett's money could not stave off the inroads of the disease. The dying youth begged to be taken back to Bluff Point, to the family's summer home in the vineyard country where he had spent so many happy days.

On July 12, 1931, a year after his death, the Garrett Memorial Chapel on the heights was consecrated and deeded to the Episcopal Church. It is commonly known as "The Chapel on the Mount." Every detail of the shrine is symbolic. On its ridge is a weather vane in the form of a ship, its sails loosed to the winds. Each chapel window depicts an incident in the life of Christ. On the silver bronze door of the crypt are symbolized the varied activities of man. Familiar poems known to youth are represented on the stained windows of the crypt.

Few colleges have so picturesque a campus as that of Keuka College for women, four miles Southwest of Penn Yan and fronting the lake for half a mile. Its 600 acres, including a farm and a wooded game sanctuary, extend up vine-clad slopes. Surrounding the campus is Keuka Park, a pleasant community with its own postoffice where many members of the faculty live.

Keuka College was born of the energy and determination of a Freewill Baptist minister, the Rev. George H. Ball. In 1887 he conceived the idea of a college in Western New York "for the Christian education of young people of both sexes." He prospected Keuka Lake by boat looking for a suitable site. He found it but lacked the necessary funds. Finally he raised $50,000 almost singlehanded.

Built from bricks made on the premises, the first building, the four-story structure known today as Ball Memorial Hall, was completed. First called Keuka Institute, the school received a provisional charter in 1892, with Dr. Ball as first president.

Activities of the school were suspended for lack of funds from 1915 to 1921. Then the school was reopened as a college for women under direction of the Northern Baptist Convention. Since then the skies have been brighter over Keuka. New buildings have been added. The college draws its students from many states. Keuka, on her sylvan, lake-washed campus, has an air of wholesome and refreshing simplicity in a chaotic world.

The temperament of the Crooked Lake is naturally serene and genial. But she has her moods. About them has been woven this old Indian legend, as told by R. B. Oldfield, veteran Steuben County Clerk:

Once many years ago in the moon of the strawberry harvest, a young Seneca was crossing the lake with his wife and young child. A sudden tempest smote the waters, capsizing the canoe. The woman and child sank from sight before the brave could rescue them. The storm passed as quickly as it came. The lake calmed but there was no sign of wife or child. Then an empty canoe drifted in with the wind. On shore a heart-broken Indian shook his fist at the lake and pronounced upon it this curse:

"Today you have seemed to smile. Your eyes laughed when my child and my wife dipped their fingers in your waters. You seemed to join us in thanking the Great Spirit that Summer had come and that the ice on your back had melted.

"But you lied. You are a snake. You have taken my family. Therefore I curse you always to be hungry when the fifth moon is in the sky. You will catch helpless women and children. For you will be hungry for them. I curse you to be unable to eat them. They will come to the top of the water and the wind will blow them to shore. I curse you always to be hungry when the fifth moon glows in the sky and the strawberries are ripe in the dark woods."

When Summer squalls bring tragedy to Keuka Lake, 'tis said the bodies always drift into shore.

132

The last rafter had been nailed fast. The frame of the new barn stood, gaunt and aromatic of freshly cut pine, against a background of green woods.

Philemon Baldwin, lithe and determined, sprang up a ladder and mounted to the ridge pole. He looked down upon a little circle of tanned faces, for the whole community had turned out for the barn raising. He spoke and his voice rang out, clear and strong:

"Men, don't you think it is time we ceased this senseless bickering over the name of this settlement? Unofficially it is called Union but you don't relish the name. Heaven knows we have little unity. You folks from Pennsylvania want recognition for your home state. You Yankees want a name that will remind you of New England. So you have wrangled and stirred up such a fuss that our neighbors laugh at us and call this place, 'Pandemonium.' Let's end this squabbling with a name that should please everyone. Let us call this future city by the Crooked Lake Penn Yan—Penn for the Pennsylvanians and Yan for the Yankees."

There was a moment of silence as the settlers thought over the compromise. Then a shout of approval arose. And that is how the comely village, that is a little city, by the Crooked Lake got its unusual name.

Pandemonium could not last long, even in early Penn Yan. It is foreign to her nature. She is practical, progressive, orderly, efficient, a mighty comfortable sort of town under her canopy of trees. Villagers and people in from the country to trade stop and visit on the sidewalks. There is always time to be neighborly.

Penn Yan's setting is picturesque. Mighty hills hem her in

on three sides. On the south stretches the long eastern arm of Keuka Lake.

This village of some 5,500 is a trading center for 35,000 people in one of the richest farm and fruit belts in the state. In frontier days she loomed large on the commercial horizon as a canal and lake port. Later, as a center of the grape and wine industry, she was an important railroad shipping point. The motor age changed that.

Penn Yan's first settlers came before the curtain rose on history. On the village site have been unearthed remains of mound-building people, definitely pre-Seneca.

To Shay's Bay State rebellion, Penn Yan owes her first white settler. In 1787 the debt-ridden farmers of Massachusetts rose against the rulers of the state. When the revolt was put down, one of its leaders, Jacob Fredenburg, fled into the wilds and found refuge with the Senecas who lived near the present site of Penn Yan. He built a log hut beside Jacob's Brook and was adopted into the tribe.

The village's growth stems from the advent of David Wagener, a follower of Jemima Wilkinson. He came from Montgomery County in 1791 after buying an interest in the Friend's Mill, the first business venture of the Jemimakins on their site near Dresden. Five years later Wagener bought land at the foot of the lake. He erected the first grist mill. His sons, Abraham and Melchoir, joined him and Abraham is revered as the father of the village. He built the first frame house and the first inn, the Mansion House, on the site of the present Knapp House. In the orchard in its rear he developed the Wagener apple. He gave Court House Square. In 1830 he built the manor house atop Bluff Point.

Traffic on the lake and on the Crooked Lake Canal brought early prosperity to the village. Flour mills and saw mills were numerous. There were several distilleries. One of the pioneer distillers named his daughter Temperance.

Penn Yan has been the county seat since the inception of Yates County in 1824. The present jail is on the site of one that was burned in 1857 by a prisoner awaiting trial—for arson.

The Iron Horse came to Keuka's shores in 1850 when ground was broken for the Canandaigua and Corning Railroad, now part of the Pennsylvania system. The next year saw 1,000 men laying tracks from Penn Yan to Watkins Glen. "Old 94" made the first run over the 46 miles in two hours, an amazing record for those days.

Eighty-two years ago when horse thieving was common, the Union Detective Club was organized. The anti-horse thief society still is a going concern, with six members and a tidy sum in the bank, although a horse thief has not operated in Yates County for a generation.

Once Penn Yan and Hammondsport vied as grape-growing centers. Those were the days when the Grape Specials steamed out of Penn Yan, sometimes 10 a day, in the Fall over the Northern Central and Fall Brook rail lines. Grapes which had come down the lake in steamboats were shipped out in five and 10-pound baskets. The label "Keuka" on a basket of grapes was a brand of excellence. Now Keuka grapes are mostly made into vintage wines and Hammondsport has become the capital of the Grape Belt.

Penn Yan never put all her eggs in one basket, not even a grape basket. She makes and sends out a lot of other things, including baskets, boats and buckwheat. Here is a substantial and busy town.

It also is a circus town, the general offices and winter quarters of "The Great James M. Cole Circus." Its proprietor, Jimmy Cole of Penn Yan, has been in the circus business all his adult life. For the last decade, except for a period of war service, he has had his own show. As this is written, his circus is touring Iowa and Nebraska. His 9-year-old son, James, Jr., "Sonny Cole, the world's youngest elephant trainer," is its star. Come snowfall, the Coles and their gaily painted wagons will be back in Penn Yan, ready for the Winter indoor circuit.

*   *   *

Until recent years whenever there was a parade in Penn Yan, a curious old carriage with a crescent shaped body had a place of honor. Once it was a proud equipage. The tapestry was the color of burnished gold. On its back panels still visible are the engraved letters, "U F." They stood for Universal Friend. It was in this coach that Jemima Wilkinson, "the woman who rose from the dead," rode all the way from Philadelphia to her new Jerusalem in the Lakes Country in 1790. Two years before her scouts had prepared a place for her.

No frontier ever knew a stranger character than the Friend. The daughter of a humble Rhode Island family arose from a seizure of brain fever to announce that she had died, that her carnal existence had ended, her body had been reanimated by the Divine Spirit and that she had returned to

136

earth, neither man nor woman, but the "Publik Unuversal Friend," to save sinners from eternal wrath.

She was unlettered but she had a magnetic way with her and the fire of a zealot. And she had business acumen. She drew followers from all over the East, some of them rich and influential. They desired a colony of their own, in some remote spot, where Jemima could rule, unmolested. They first chose a site near Dresden. Nearby they built the first mill and harvested the first wheat sown west of Seneca Lake.

The settlement, first in the region, thrived and added to its holdings. Around 1790 the Friend moved to a new site, a hill near Branchport, on the Shearman Hollow Road, within sight of the Crooked Lake. There after five years in the building rose the staunch, three-story clapboard house of hand-hewn timbers and with nine fireplaces that stands today and is known as "The Friend's House."

Jemima ruled with an iron hand. She forbade her subjects to marry but some of them disobeyed. She controlled the finances of her colony. She made friends with the Indians. She disapproved of the gay goings-on in Charles Williamson's town of Bath, with its taverns, theater and horse races. The Friend preached a simple doctrine: If you were good, you went to heaven. If you sinned and did not repent, you burned in hell fire.

The prophetess died or as she phrased it "left time," in 1819. Without its forceful leader, the sect gradually disintegrated. There are many descendants of the Jemimakins left in the neighborhood. They are thrifty, substantial people. The burial place of The Friend is known to but two people. It is a secret handed down through generations.

137

Arnold Potter of Penn Yan is one who knows. He will never tell.

In the Penn Yan Library is a well worn saddle of fine leather, trimmed with silver. There also is a whip, frayed as if with much use and a straight-backed old-fashioned chair. They are carefully preserved, for once they belonged to the Friend. Her coach was recently presented by its last owner, Miss Velma Remer of Penn Yan, to the Wood Memorial Library and Museum in Canandaigua.

For years the Friend's House was allowed to run down. For seven years it was vacant. Then Mr. and Mrs. Joseph E. Florance of Hornell purchased the place and they have restored it to its old-time grandeur. It glistens on its hilltop in a fresh coat of white paint. The original white pine floors, the cherry stair railing, the fireplaces made from brick on the premises, the balcony above the hall from where Jemima addressed her people, the upper chambers where her hand maidens dwelt, the crypt outside where she lay in state for three days awaiting the resurrection, and which now stores vegetables—over all of them hovers the spirit of The Universal Friend.

In fancy she rides over the countryside again, a woman dressed both like man and like woman, with flashing dark eyes and raven ringlets that hang down over a white scarf knotted around her strong neck, one of the most remarkable women ever to live in the Finger Lakes Country.

*   *   *

A stranger, driving along the Bath-Hammondsport road, once said to his companion, a native of the region:

138

"My, this is a pleasant valley. What is its name?"

"Pleasant Valley," was the reply.

The pioneers first gave it that name. For there the grass seemed to be greener and the skies bluer than anywhere else in this raw young land. And the steep slopes around the head of Keuka Lake seemed to catch more than their share of sunshine.

The lovely basin scooped out of the hills has had several names. One of them was Cold Spring Valley because of the icy water that flowed there.

The village that grew up at the head of the lake and of the valley for more than a century has borne the name of Hammondsport, after Lazarus Hammond, an early settler.

After men had planted vines on the sunny hillsides and found that the grapes that grew there made the finest wines in the land, the place came to be known as the Grape Bowl of the East.

And when early in the new century, strange, birdlike contraptions began to flutter over the lake and the vineyards, it got another name, the Cradle of Aviation. That was because a native son, Glenn Hammond Curtiss, a pioneer of the skyways and the father of naval aviation, lived and worked there.

Glenn Curtiss was an unusual man but not in appearance. He was thin and he had a prominent Adam's apple and he grew bald early in life. He detested speech making and ceremony and he had not an iota of showmanship in his makeup. He had no formal engineering education yet top engineers and scientists sought his advice and followed his roughly drawn plans. A dreamer, intent on discovering

139

swifter and safer ways of travel, he was yet a doer and saw most of his dreams come true. Generous and often the prey of cranks and swindlers, he amassed a fortune.

Bicycles were his first love. He had a little repair and sales shop in Hammondsport and there devised a bicycle which he called the Hercules. Later on he added a motor to his bike and began making motocycle engines. He raced his own motorcycles and won two world's records.

In 1903, the year of the Wright brothers' epochal flight, Curtiss started making motors for balloons. He received many orders, including one from the United States government, its first timid step in the path of military aeronautics.

With Alexander Graham Bell, inventor of the telephone, and others, Curtiss carried on in Hammondsport the pioneer work of the Aerial Experimental Association, which resulted in the first airplane flight in New York State.

It was on March 2, 1908 that the Red Wing, a crate-like contraption with a single thickness of red silk covering two kite-like wings, with beams and struts built of spruce and with a 24 horsepower, eight cylinder Curtiss motor, was placed on the flat top of a grape-hauling barge, three miles up icy-mantled Keuka Lake. With F. W. "Casey" Baldwin at the stick, the thing actually flew 318 feet. Then it capsized on the ice like a wounded duck.

On the Fourth of July in 1908 the slopes of Pleasant Valley were black with people. The magazine, Scientific American, had offered a trophy to the first American pilot to fly one kilometer (0.621 miles). Curtiss and his associates built the June Bug, a new ship, for this test. After waiting hours "until the wind was right," Curtiss flew the "crate" nearly a mile and the cup was his. Hammondsport was the scene of the first public, pre-announced airplane flight in America.

Curtiss' prestige rose. The little shop near his home that had started in 1901 with three hands, employed 300. Later on, the June Bug was fitted with pontoons and alighted many times on the lake. That was the birth of naval aviation.

In 1909 Curtiss received the first order for an airplane ever given an American manufacturer. That year he won the International Speed Race in Rheims, France, and when he came home, a 20-man team of his neighbors pulled his carriage through the streets of his home village under a hastily built arch of triumph.

Forever setting precedents, Curtiss in 1911 opened the first flying school in America in Hammondsport. His students came from many lands. They dashed about the dusty roads in rakish cars. They danced all hours in the pavilions along the lake. There were gay parties at the homes of the wine magnates. Those years were the maddest the lakeside village had ever known.

About the same time Curtiss organized his Flying Circus and to Hammondsport came such pioneer barnstormers as Lincoln Beachey, Beckwith Havens and Eugene Ely. Curtiss built flying boats. Wealthy sportsmen like William Thaw and Harold McCormick came, took lessons and bought planes.

The eyes of the world were on little Hammondsport in 1914. First, the pioneer Langley plane, symbol of a great defeat, was brought from Washington to be reconditioned and flown in a scientific demonstration that stirred up much controversy. Then Curtiss built a flying boat for rich Rodman Wanamaker, designed to span the Atlantic for a $50,000 prize. The boat never flew because the world went to war at just the time it was to take off from Canada.

The war brought an immediate boom to the village. Curtiss was just developing his famous tractor biplane, JN or "Jenny," in which so many World War 1 flyers were trained. The Curtiss plant had outgrown the village and he bought and built large factories in Buffalo. The Hammondsport plant roared night and day with 3,000 employes, thrice the village population.

The Armistice ended the aviation boom. Prohibition crippled the wine industry. The village sank back into slumber. Curtiss traveled much but spent all his spare time at the homestead on the hill which still stands but moved a bit to make way for the fine Curtiss Memorial School, of which it is a part. Whenever Curtiss signed a hotel register, whether in New York, Paris or London, it always was as "G. H. Curtiss, Hammondsport N. Y."

His funeral was the biggest Hammondsport ever knew. Noted scientists, aviators, industrialists mingled with villagers who had watched the boy who could fix bicycles and repair door bells rise to the heights of fame.

* * *

Omar Khayyam would have felt at home in "The Grape Bowl of the East."

He would have enjoyed Keuka's sapphire radiance and the smell of the grapes ripening in the Autumn sunshine. The old Tentmaker would have liked the serene old village, too, its shady square and its quiet streets.

But most of all, he who sang of the Vine would have loved the cool, cavernous depths of the great, stone-walled wine cellars, some of them set like baronial castles, back into the hillsides. He could watch the trucks roll up, piled high with sweet Delawares, Catawbas, Concords, Elviras, Isabellas. He would have made friends with the jolly wine makers, their white frocks stained a gaudy purple. He would have been fascinated by the huge vats and casks, the rows of bottles on the racks. And the all-pervading, heady odor of the grape in ferment would have warmed his convivial soul.

There is the air of an older world about this valley where the days are warm and sunny and the nights are cool and clear and the grapes are sweetest grown. The vineyard capital, Hammondsport, is unlike any other Lakes Country community. Her wine cellars have generated an open-handed, expansive way of life along Keuka's shores.

The Keuka grape industry had its beginnings in an Episcopal rector's garden. Around 1840 the Rev. William Bostwick of Hammondsport sent to the Hudson Valley for slips of the Isabella and Catawba varieties. He planted them on the rectory grounds and they flourished in the saintly soil.

The good rector did not commercialize his vineyard but other growers did. In 1847 the first shipment of Keuka grapes, 50 pounds, went to the New York market, from the terraced vineyard of William Hastings overlooking the lake. In 1857 J. M. Prentiss shipped a ton of grapes from his

Pulteney farm. By 1860 there were 200 acres of vineyard around the lake.

That year the French vintner, Charles D. Champlin, came to Pleasant Valley. He discovered that this Western New York countryside closely paralleled the famous vineyard belt around Rheims, France, in climate, soil and drainage and was ideal for the growing of vintage grapes.

It was blessed with an abundance of sunshine in the maturing months, a minimum of insects and fungi. The hills provided a natural shelter, the Fall winds wafted over Keuka were warmish and the frosts came late. All of these factors made the grapes grown in "the American Rhineland" of high sugar content.

In 1861 Champlin established the first winery in the Keuka area and was granted U. S. Winery License No. 1, still held by the Pleasant Valley Wine Company he founded. Another big operator is Taylor Bros., founded in 1880.

The industry thrived after the Civil War. In 1889 there were 14,000 acres of vineyards around Keuka. In the late 1890s the acreage had reached 25,000. In those days six steamboats and many tow barges hauled the grapes down the lake and sometimes six trains a day rumbled out of Hammondsport on the ten-mile-long Bath and Hammondsport Railroad. The little road is still in operation and its red cabooses bear the name of "The Champagne Route." About all it hauls is wine.

Prohibition struck a staggering blow at the wine industry, one from which it has never entirely recovered although grape growing still is the major industry of the Hammondsport region.

144

Vineyarding entails plenty of work and eternal vigilance. Plowing, dragging, spraying against pests, hoeing, trimming of vines, replacing and driving posts, tieing the shoots with willow twigs to keep them straight and later on the main vines with straw binding—these are some of the routine operations that rob grape raising of glamor.

The harvest is a stupendous affair. Armies of men and women cut the clusters from the vines with knives and shears and place them in 40-pound boxes to be trucked to the wineries.

There, after the pressing and early fermentation processes, the juice is bottled. Champagne making is a four-year process. The bottles rest on their sides for a year before being put on racks and the sediment removed. Brandy syrup is added to give the proper sweetness. The bottles are corked and wired and put on shelves before they are turned—by hand twice a day for a year. One man turns thousands of bottles daily and he does it deftly, using both hands at the same time.

The cool, vaulted wine cellars are intriguing places, with their mammoth storage tanks, miles of tube which carry the crimson liquid from one process to another, huge rooms stacked with bottles. At certain stages of the fermentation process, workers wear masks like fencers to protect their faces against possible explosion of the bottles.

*   *   *

East of Keuka's southern shores two little "Finger Lakes" sparkle in the hills 1,000 feet above the level of the sea. They are Waneta, once called Little Lake, three miles long with its foot near the village of Wayne, and Lamoka, to the south, shorter but wider. Mud Lake was Lamoka's old name.

Near Lamoka archeologists have unearthed remains of a prehistoric Indian occupation, believed to be the oldest in the state and antedating the discoveries on Frontenac Island.

The Tyrone region was the scene of a natural gas boom in the 1920s but the field was exhausted in a few years. About the same time grandiose plans were launched for a power development tapping the little lakes and building a canal to Keuka but that, too, failed of fruition.

Between the two mountain lakes and Keuka is the Aisle of Pines. That is what once was a magnificent estate, set among aisles of lofty pine trees.

Chances are you'd whiz right by the Aisle of Pines without noticing it unless you spotted the massive gates, the gate-keeper's lodge and the long silent fountain at the entrance.

Samuel Hallett, a native son who became a railroad builder in the West and was slain by a discharged employe on the streets of Wyandotte, Kans., built the big house in the 1860s, close to the road. Around 1900 George K. Birge, Buffalo industrialist, leased the estate and moved the house back on the hill. He spent a small fortune on the place, even building a private race track. People in Wayne for years could find work at "The Big House," for Birge was forever lavishing money on it.

After Birge's death some 25 years ago, the estate fell into disuse and disrepair. The Big House with its 24 massive stone pillars, its distinguished Southern plantation style of architecture and tall windows, their panes smashed by vandals, is a desolate sight today. The once fine lawns are covered with underbrush and the flower gardens are untended.

The place even has its private cemetery. In a corner of the grounds under a canopy of pines sleep Samuel Hallett, the railroad builder, and members of his family. Towering above the headstones is a monument 35 feet high.

The Aisle of Pines estate itself is a monument to a glory that has departed.

Chapter 10

Canandaigua, "The Chosen Place"

Canandaigua is an Indian Name and it means "The Chosen Place."

It is the name of the most westerly of the Finger Lakes and of a historic city at the foot of that long and lovely lake. It is a proud name in the annals of two nations.

Above Canandaigua's waters is the legendary birthplace of the Seneca Indians, "The People of the Hill." In all the forest empire of the mightiest nation of the Iroquois Confederacy no place was more revered.

The city that the pioneers built on the site of an old Indian village became "The Chosen Place" of the white men too. It has always been a seat of government, the place where treaties were made, where affairs of state were settled, where the black-robed judges sat.

It was the capital of a vast frontier when Rochester was a fever-plagued swamp, when Buffalo was an Indian village, when Syracuse was a salt marsh.

At Canandaigua was established the first office for the sale of land directly to settlers in America, marking the beginning of settlement west of Seneca Lake. It was the shire town of "The Mother of Counties" when Ontario embraced all that is now Western New York. The dome of its Court

House, glistening above the trees and visible for miles in any direction, is its oriflamme.

Canandaigua's broad principal street, lined with majestic trees, noble public buildings and time-mellowed mansions, bears witness to the dreams of the founders who planned a great city there.

It was a stage on which was enacted much of the drama of the frontier. The actors were the great ones of their time. Cabinet members, generals, senators, jurists, landed gentry, land promoters, Seneca chieftains, prophets of new religions were in that cast.

Two remarkable women, Jemima Wilkerson, founder of a fantastic cult, and Susan B. Anthony, crusader for women's rights, faced Canandaigua's courts in bold defense of their beliefs. When William Morgan was abducted from her old jail, the Anti-Masonic party was born and the whole land thrown into ferment. Louis Philippe of France, Charles Williamson, Timothy Pickering, Phelps and Gorham, Gideon and Francis Granger, Stephen A. Douglas—those are some of the glittering names in her long, proud history.

It came to pass that the Erie Canal and the Main Line of the New York Central Railroad swung to the northward and Canandaigua was denied her early dreams of commercial glory. But she remained the Grand Dame of the Finger Lakes. She is a stately and serene dowager and holds her head high. Yet she is friendly withal. Her position is so secure in history she needs curry favor with none. The charm of an old regime still invests this city by the long blue lake.

Almost every corner of Canandaigua yields its vision of the past.

At the foot of the lake stood a neat Indian village called Kanandague with the most modern and best built log houses in the land of the Senecas—until Sullivan's army came in 1779 and left it in charred ruins.

Nine years later a log store house rose in the woods. A New England syndicate, headed by Oliver Phelps and Nathaniel Gorham, had brought two million acres of wilderness and Canandaigua was "the chosen spot" for the headquarters of that enterprise. No one spent the winter of 1788 in that rude shelter but the next year one Joseph Smith moved in before the snow was off the ground. That was the beginning of settlement.

In a few months a party of ten, led by General Israel Chapin, arrived after a long and hazardous journey over water routes from New England. With them came 37-year-old William Walker, agent for Phelps and Gorham. A log hut rose on the Public Square near the present Main Street railroad crossing. It was Walker's office, the first in the New World where land was sold directly to settlers.

Then two new frame houses, the first to be built west of Oneida County, attracted the admiration of the frontier. Thomas Morris, son of Robert Morris, owner of vast lands, lived in one, Oliver Phelps in the other. In the old Pioneer Cemetery is a box-like tomb that marks Oliver Phelps' last resting place. Before he died, much of his wilderness empire had passed into other hands. He sleeps in good company. Many another pioneer is in that old burying ground. The inscriptions on some of the headstones have been obliterated by time.

One of the old stones marks the grave of Caleb Walker.

It was the first one dug there. There was no clergyman available in 1790, so a physician, Dr. William Adams of Geneva, intoned the words of the Episcopal prayer service and led the procession to the grave. For 90 years thereafter, until the custom was abolished at the earnest behest of the medical society, the attending physician led all funeral processions in Canandaigua.

The year of 1794 was a stirring one in the frontier capital. For weeks Indians had been pouring into the village, setting up their tents on the lakeshore and in the woods. Tall Timothy Pickering came as the agent of the Great White Father, to sign a treaty with the Senecas and establish boundaries and settle claims for all time. Back of the festivities, the horse racing, the dancing and the oratory around the council fires, tension gripped the negotiators. In Ohio "Mad Anthony" Wayne's American army was meeting the western Indians. On the outcome of that battle rode the fate of the frontier. In the event of Wayne's defeat, the Senecas were ready for the warpath, led by their British friends. A runner brings good news. Wayne has won. And the chastened Seneca chiefs hasten to sign the treaty.

The Indians reveled in gifts of broadcloth and blankets, silver trinkets and beads. Someone slipped them forbidden firewater. Then the nights were made hideous with war whoops and brawling. Even after the signing of the treaty, the Senecas lingered, displaying their new finery.

The treaty, signed against that fantastic backdrop, was of historic importance. It was the basic agreement between the Senecas and the United States and its terms have never been abrogated. It confirmed the Phelps and Gorham purchase

151

and settled the Indian claims, with the proviso that "The United States will never disturb the Seneca Nation." That promise was not fully kept.

A boulder near Ontario County's stately Court House commemorates the signing of the Pickering Treaty and the last general council with the Senecas. And in the Wood Memorial Library and Museum is a faded old parchment always kept under lock and key. It is the Indians' copy of the original Pickering Treaty. Handed down from sachem to sachem, it finally came into a white collector's hands and then into the Canandaigua archives. It bears the names of famous chiefs, Red Jacket, Cornplanter, Handsome Lake, Farmer's Brother, Little Beard, Fish Carrier. Each signed with a cross.

Ontario County's old jail, which went down in 1895, was the scene of a historic "kidnaping" in 1826. In that old jail behind a high stone wall was lodged on a trumped-up charge a stone mason with a defiant, dissolute face. His name was William Morgan. Back of his arrest for a $2 debt was his threat to expose the secrets of Free Masonry. Men, no friends of Morgan, came to the jail, paid the $2 debt and took the prisoner into their keeping one moonlight September night. Frenzied cries were heard as Morgan was seized, bound, gagged and thrown into a waiting carriage with drawn curtains.

Then began a strange journey across the state to Fort Niagara. There all trace of William Morgan disappeared. Foes of Free Masonry raised a fierce tempest and astute politicians seized upon the agitation to found the Anti-Masonic Party, which played a brief but exciting role in national politics.

Canandaigua's Stately Court House

Steamboat Days on Conesus

Memories, glorious and grim, haunt the old mansions and other old buildings of the town. Hidden away behind a store in Coy Street are the remains of probably Canandaigua's oldest house. It was built in the 1790s by General Chapin, the peacemaker with the Indians.

Well back from Main Street under spreading trees and with a generous sweep of lawn stands the three-story Granger Homestead in its warm coat of yellow paint. Gideon Granger, postmaster-general under two Presidents, built the mansion in 1814. It is said his friend, Thomas Jefferson, had a hand in its planning. Certainly its noble, simple lines have a Jeffersonian touch.

After Gideon, his son, Francis Granger, lived there. He was an unsuccessful candidate for the Vice Presidency and was postmaster-general under William Henry Harrison. He led a faction of the Whig Party that tried to de-emphasize the slavery issue. Because of Granger's long gray locks, this group was called "The Silver Grays." From 1875 to 1906 the mansion was the Granger Place School for young ladies. Then the Granger family lived there until 1929 when Miss Antoinette, last of the clan and a lady of the old school, died.

Under her will it became a home for retired Congregationalist ministers and their wives. In 1945 the church decided to close the home and the historic homestead faced possible demolition. Public spirited Canandaiguans formed a non-profit membership corporation and bought the house. Now it is preserved for posterity and open to the public, with all its wealth of old time furnishings, as a fine example of a post Colonial American home.

Around the 150-year old residence at 210 North Main Street clings the aura of great names and a tale of tragedy. It was built by Gen. Peter B. Porter, the defender of Black Rock in the War of 1812 and a one-time secretary of war. In later years John C. Spencer, who held the treasury and war portfolios under President Tyler, lived there. More recently the old house was the residence of Elbridge G. Lapham, who served in the United States Senate.

In that house a son, Philip, was born in 1821 to the John C. Spencers. He grew into a tall, handsome daredevil with a sinister cast in one eye. When he was 21 years old and while his father was secretary of war, Philip Spencer sailed on the U. S. navy brig Somers as a midshipman. On the return cruise from Africa, a steward poured into the ear of the captain, Alexander Slidell Mackenzie, the tale of a plot aboard ship to mutiny, murder the officers, seize the ship and hoist the black flag. The leader of the plot, the steward said, was the son of the secretary of war.

A council of ship's officers doomed young Spencer and two other conspirators to death. One gray afternoon in December, 1842, the crew of the Somers averted their faces from the yardarm where dangled the bodies of three of their comrades. One of them was Philip Spencer of Canandaigua. The execution created a national sensation. The powerful Spencers and their friends claimed the sentence was hasty, unmerited and the crime unproved. When the Somers docked at New York, her captain faced a federal inquiry and a Naval court martial. Mackenzie was exonerated but bitter feelings over the affair persisted for years.

Canandaigua Academy has always kept the old fashioned name the pioneers gave it when the first school was built in 1795. Some famous names have been on the rolls of the Academy. One was Stephen Arnold Douglas who enrolled when he was 17 and a newcomer from Vermont. After three years he went West, to become "The Little Giant" of national politics and the rival in debate and for the Presidency of Abraham Lincoln.

A landmark is the 139-year-old First Congregational Church with its quaint "built-in" porch under a half moon arch. For years its bell led the Sunday morning chorus of church chimes in deference to its age.

Canandaigua has had three court houses. The first one, adorned with a codfish weather vane, was erected in 1794. There Jemima Wilkinson, the Universal Friend, faced a charge of blasphemy of which she was acquitted. There Red Jacket, according to tradition, appearing as counsel for an accused Indian, defeated his rival, a white attorney.

The second court house, now the City Hall, served from 1824 to 1857 when the present stately building with the shining dome was erected. In 1872 a square-jawed spinster faced a federal judge in its courtroom from whose walls the pictured faces of the pioneers look down. The prisoner at the bar was Susan B. Anthony, accused of the crime of casting her vote in defiance of the law. She had led a little band of women through a gaping crowd of men in a Rochester polling place to demand and be granted the right to cast their ballots. The federal judge directed a verdict of guilty and denied defense counsel's plea that the case be given to the jury. The suffrage leader, who had wanted to go to jail for cause, was fined $100—which she never paid. There's a story that the night after her trial the wooden statue of Justice atop the gilded dome came down in a high wind.

In that same courthouse 65 years later the first woman juror in Western New York's history was sworn into service.

The shire town has bred some notable lawyers and politicos. One was John Raines, Civil War commander, state senator, congressman and Republican boss of Ontario County, a power in his time. He was the author of the Raines Law which increased the tax on all hotels serving liquor. It also provided that only bona fide hotels could serve intoxicants on Sundays. Every place that sold intoxicants sought to come under the "hotel" definition. As a result "Raines Law hotels" became common, places which contained beds in which none slept and sandwiches which none ate. Sometimes a lone and mouldy sandwich, which had been on exhibit for months, sufficed. These abuses were not the fault of the author of the law which was repealed.

In those days the Democratic boss was John Flanagan but he is remembered, not as a politician but for the fine food he served, especially the 25 cent oyster stews. His restaurant once was famous throughout the state. He began his career peddling sandwiches at the railroad station. Celebrated, too, at the dawn of the century and later was Canandaigua ale, made in the old McKechnie brewery.

In 1890 a tall smiling youth named John N. Willys opened a bicycle shop on Main Street. He had mechanical skill and business acumen and he went on to power and riches in the infant automobile industry, rounding out his career as ambassador to Poland. Other notables who called

Canandaigua home in their youth have been Max Eastman, the radical writer-lecturer and Sidney Smith, the cartoonist. A Canandaiguan once sued Smith, claiming that creator of comic strips had used him as the model for his "Andy Gump."

Canandaigua had its Lady Bountiful, too. She was Mrs. Frederick Ferris Thompson and she was the daughter of Myron H. Clark, only Prohibitionist ever elected governor of New York. She was immensely wealthy and gave to her home city, a site for the postoffice, a hospital and laboratory and a civic playground.

The Thompson estate, Sonnenberg, was for years a show place of the city. There was a pretentious mansion on the 612 acres and woods, rose gardens, sunken gardens, lawns, greenhouses, an aviary of 500 birds, a 400-gallon swimming pool and a view of Canandaigua Lake.

Today that former estate is the site of a United States Veterans' Hospital for neuro-psychiatric cases arising from war. It was opened in 1933 and its original cost was $1,700,000 after its sale to the government by Mrs. Thompson's heirs. The former mansion is now a nurses' home. Veterans of three wars have been cared for at the VA hospital, which with its sizeable payroll constitutes a major Canandaigua industry.

A city since 1913, Canandaigua is the third smallest in the state with a population of about 8,300. Only Sherril and Mechanicville are smaller. There were those who opposed Canandaigua's attaining the status of a city. Those same influences have tended to keep it a fine residential city without too much smoke staining the historic buildings.

In later years people from Rochester and other places have been buying the old mansions and moving in. They have infused some new blood into the old city but they aren't going to change Canandaigua over night. She has been a Grand Dame too long and her traditions are too deeply rooted. You cannot blame her too much for glorying in her past. For that past has been glorious.

*　　*　　*

Canandaigua Lake on clear days mirrors the sky and the wooded hills, rich with vineyards on the gentler slopes and rising to wild heights at its head. But the lake has its angry moods when the water turns a steely gray and caps of white ride the tossing waves.

On such mornings when the wind charges down from South Hill like a galloping buffalo and whips the lake into fury, those who believe in legends say, "It's the 10 o'clock wash. The Great Serpent is turning over in the bottom of the lake."

They mean the reptillian monster that centuries ago all but exterminated the Senecas, "The People of the Great Hill." The legend of the Serpent of Bare Hill has several versions. Here is one of them:

Long ago the Creator caused the earth to open and out of the side of a massive hill the ancestors of the Seneca Nation came into being. For a time they lived in peace there. Then a boy of the tribe found a little snake in the woods. It was an unusual serpent for it had two heads. The boy took it home, made a pet of it and fed it the choicest deer meat. The thing grew to incredible size and its hunger knew no bounds. Its master could not obtain enough game for it. The people of the tribe came to fear it as a monster.

Finally the great snake encircled the hill and barred the gate with its opened double jaws. Driven by hunger, the trapped people tried to get away and one by one, they were eaten by the Thing. At last a young warrior and his sister were all that remained of the People of the Hill.

One night the young brave had a vision. If he would fletch his arrows with his sister's hair, they would possess a fatal charm over the enemy. He followed his dream and shot his magic arrows straight into the serpent's heart. The reptile was mortally hurt and in agony writhed his way down Bare Hill, tearing out trees and flailing the earth until he finally slid into the lake.

As the snake rolled down the hill, he disgorged the skulls of the Senecas he had devoured. In the area have been found large rounded stones divided into geometric patterns, some of them weirdly like human heads. The superstitious Indians knew nothing of the science of geology which defines the pattern of the stones as formed by the slow deposit of lime in the post-glacial age.

But to this day nothing has grown in the path of the snake down old Bare Hill. Its somber head stands out above the rich and fruitful Vine Valley. Fertilizing the soil does no good. The hill is just as bare as it was when the white men first saw it.

Again science has an explanation for the hill's sterility. It is covered with shale so thick that rain cannot soak in and refresh the soil.

For years Bare Hill has been pointed out as the legendary

birthplace of the Seneca Nation. But Dr. Arthur C. Parker, director emeritus of the Rochester Museum and former state archeologist, believes otherwise. He is an outstanding authority on the Six Nations. In his veins flows the blood of the Keepers of the Western Door. He is a descendant of Red Jacket. While he "hates to spoil a picturesque legend," he maintains that excavations have proved that South Hill or Sunnyside in the Whaleback country, and not Bare Hill, was occupied by the early Senecas. He says Bare Hill was the home of an earlier people. Sunnyside presents the same phenomenon of bareness as does Bare Hill.

When Doctor Parker retired from his museum position, he chose his home on a lofty eminence known locally as "Rumpus Hill," because of early feuds and barn burnings there. It's tranquil enough today. The view of the lake and the hills at its head is superb. And from his study window the descendant of Red Jacket can look out at the nearby hill which he firmly believes is the real birthplace of the Seneca Nation.

Around tiny Squaw Island at the foot of the lake hangs another Indian legend. It is said that when Sullivan's army approached, the Seneca women and children sought refuge on the tree-clad isle. Now the smallest of New York state parks, about half an acre, it diminishes each year as the lake eats into its shores.

Sullivan's troopers reported finding wild grapes in profusion in the present Vine Valley. They were precursors of the present large vineyards there. No doubt the weary soldiers caught their breath as motorists do today when at a turn of the road, the blue splendor of the lake suddenly unfolds and it seems as if the highway were about to leap into the water.

In 1823 a pretty maid in a demure bonnet and gay ribbon smashed a bottle of wine over the side of the first boat to sail Canandaigua Lake. She was Sally, daughter of Thomas Morris. The boat with sails was the Lady of the Lake and it was built by Canandaigua capital.

Then followed many a steamboat on the lake. There were the two Ontarios, the first one launched in 1845; the Henry D. Gibson, built 20 years later; the Joseph Wood, the first of the side wheelers; the Canandaigua; the Genundewah, which burned at the Woodville dock in 1894; the three boats of the Canandaigua Lake Steamship Company, the big Onnalinda, which carried 600 passengers on Summer Sundays, with another 400 on a boat in tow; the Ogarita, which had the shrillest whistle on the lake and which because of her Irish crew was dubbed the "O'Garrity," and the Seneca Chief, a small fast craft. There also was the Oriana, built in 1889. The last of the line, the Eastern Star, was launched in 1914.

When Wally Reed, last of the lake boat captains and still a familiar figure at the foot of the lake, moored his canopy-topped Eastern Star for the last time on a Fall day in 1932, he was writing finis to more than a century of navigation on Canandaigua Lake.

Once 60 docks dotted the 32 miles of lakeline and from them the steamboats picked up grapes from Vine Valley, apples from Woodville and other produce all along the line. Above decks, bands played and passengers danced in the old excursion days. Some steamboats carried 50 to 65 tons of grapes which were transferred to the freight cars of the Pennsylvania line which ran down to the water's edge.

Now the docks are gone at the old ports of call around the lake, Glen Cove, Oak Cliff, Monteith's, Forester's Point, Bay View, Windsor Beach, Gage's, Seneca Point and the rest. Seneca Point was a popular resort where Maj. F. O. Chamberlin operated a four-story, many turreted hotel with broad porches and a dancing pavilion.

Oldtimers like John Gartland who has watched the changing scene all of his 92 years, can tell of days when the lake boats furnished virtually all the freight and passenger transport around the lake, for the roads were narrow and rough; of times when he drove all the way to Vine Valley and back to Canandaigua on the ice of the lake; of the winter ice harvests and the big ice house at the foot of the lake, of the commercial fishermen who made Canandaigua white fish almost as famous as Flanagan's oyster stews.

Canandaigua is the "Chosen Place" for hundreds of Summer residents. They come from Rochester, Buffalo, the adjoining territory and from far away places. It is popular with sailors and the home of the Canandaigua Yacht Club, perched on a hill on the West Lake Road, commands a superb view. Roseland Park at the foot of the lake along busy Routes 5–20 is the Coney Island for a large region.

On the east side of the lake is a different Summer colony. It is the Le Tourneau Christian Camp and it is centered around a tabernacle. It was founded 11 years ago by Robert G. Le Tourneau, a midwest manufacturer of road-making machinery, who promotes what he calls a "practical Christianity" based on Fundamentalist doctrines. His camp primarily is a revival center for young people. During World War 2 it housed child refugees from Europe.

*　.*　*

Three miles from the head of the lake, hemmed in by majestic hills, lies Naples, in a countryside that a great phrase-maker, William Jennings Bryan, once called "a spread of poetry written by the Great Author of the universe."

In the 1850s Edward McKay planted 150 grape vines of the Isabella variety on a hillside near Naples. It was the beginning of a big industry. Germans, who knew the science of grape growing and wine making, were attracted to the fertile countryside. One of them was Jacob Widmer. His descendants today operate in Naples one of the largest wineries in the East.

In Naples Common, the old village meeting place, stands a bronze tablet to the memory of the Indian chief, Canasque, the friend of the white settlers, who at the age of 100 was brought in a sled to die in his old home on the site of Naples village.

What was said to be the oldest tree in the world was discovered in fossil form in Grimes Glen at Naples in 1882 by the late D. Dean Luther, state geologist and a resident of the village. The restored fossil, which goes back to the Devonian period, is now in the State Museum at Albany.

East of Canandaigua Lake in picturesque valleys lie such pleasant villages as Middlesex, Gorham and Rushville. Rushville is the birthplace of one of the Lakes Country's most famous sons, Dr. Marcus Whitman. That medical missionary blazed the first wagon trail over the Rockies and helped save Oregon Territory to the Union. His wife, Narcissa Prentiss, who as a girl lived at Prattsburg in the Steuben County hills, died with Whitman in an Indian massacre in 1847.

Chapter 11

Little Finger Lakes

HONEOYE, CANADICE, HEMLOCK, CONESUS

In the upland country south of Rochester lie four "little Finger Lakes." Reading from east to west, they are Honeoye, Canadice, Hemlock and Conesus.

They differ from their eastern sisters only in size. All save Hemlock bear old Indian names. These lakes are in the Rochester orbit. Hemlock and Canadice provide the city with most of its water supply. Honeoye and Conesus provide Rochesterians with delightful Summer and year-around places to live.

Around the slim blue lake named Honeoye stretches a mystic countryside. To the east are the wild and picturesque Bristol Hills. In Autumn those hills are decked with such gorgeous colors that people travel miles for the spectacle. In Winter they are a symphony in green and white.

Yet city folk have been slow to "discover" this countryside. Now hunting cabins and summer homes stand between weather-beaten old farmhouses in the hills and the twelve miles of Honeoye Lake shore are dotted with a summer colony of 3,000 people. Ever since Hiroshima, more and more city people are taking up permanent abode in that countryside. Perhaps the distance from Rochester, regarded as an atom bomb target, has something to do with it.

At Honeoye village, at the foot of the lake that bears its name, urbanites of many bloods rub elbows with the men and women whose Yankee ancestors settled there more than 150 years ago.

Honeoye's history follows a familiar pattern. First the site of the village on the flats housed an Indian town of 20 log houses.

One September day in 1779 the Seneca old men, women and children left in the village were quietly braiding their corn and boiling their succotash when they heard the distant boom of cannon to the eastward. Sullivan's men were marching over the trail from Canandaigua. When Sullivan arrived there was not an Indian in sight. The soldiers destroyed the village and the crops.

At Honeoye the Yankee general left a garrison of 50 men with a three-pound cannon. These men built a stockade called Fort Cummings after their leader and the rest of the army marched on. In the center of the village a monument commemorates the fort built there in 1779 with the notation that "here were left the lame, the sick and the lazy" of the Sullivan Expedition.

In 1787 a group of Massachusetts men bought 46,000 acres which now embrace much of the towns of Richmond and Bristol in Ontario County. Two years later after an arduous three-month journey from the Bay State, the first settlers, led by Peter and Gideon Pitts, arrived at the flats at the foot of Honeoye Lake. The Pitts family became the leaders of the new community. Capt. Peter Pitts was a patriarch of the backwoods and the town for a time was called Pitt's Town. The Indians called the lake Honeoye, which means "finger lying," probably so named because of its shape. Later on the village took the name of the lake at its border.

The Pitts house became a stopping place for notables, the Wadsworth brothers from Geneseo, Thomas Morris and French nobility in the persons of the Duke de Liancourt and the wandering Louis Philippe, who became a king of France. Louis wrote of a Sunday sojourn in the Pitts home:

"On our arrival we found the house crowded with Presbyterians, its owners attending to a noisy, tedious harangue delivered by a minister with such violence of elocution that he appeared all over in a perspiration. There were handsome women in attendance and we found them even more pleasant than fine rural scenery."

The marriage of a daughter of the house of Pitts to Frederick Douglass, the Negro leader, caused a sensation in 1884. The bride, Mount Holyoke-educated descendant of white pioneers, was 45. Douglass, born in slavery and a widower, was in his sixties.

Helen Pitts was a child when Douglass first visited Honeoye and met her father, the second Gideon. Pitts was identified with the Underground Railroad and in his woodshed was an uncompleted excavation for a cistern which never held any water but which secreted many a fugitive. Helen Pitts went to Washington as a government employe. She became Douglass' secretary when he was made recorder of deeds for the District of Columbia. Their marriage pleased neither blacks or whites. But the couple was unruffled by the storm. Douglass said, "My first wife was the color of my mother. My second wife is the color of my father." Helen Douglass remained loyal to her Negro husband and after his death, was instrumental in founding a Douglass Memorial Association.

Honeoye Lake lacks the long Summer resort history of Conesus and Hemlock. There were no big hotels on her shores or passenger boats on her waters. Development of Honeoye as a Summer colony began only about 30 years ago and was led by Rochester people.

On a hill north of Honeoye is an almost extinct community named Allen's Hill. Once it was a thriving place with stores, churches and several distilleries. The remaining buildings include a two-room white schoolhouse under the brow of the hill.

In 1843 a 15-year-old girl came from her Massachusetts home to live with an uncle at Allen's Hill and to teach in the little school. Her name was Mary Jane Hawes. For four years she taught there. Then she married a frail young lawyer, Daniel Holmes. They lived in Kentucky for a year. Then she came back to Allen's Hill to teach for a short time. The couple moved to Canandaigua and eventually to Brockport, where Mary Jane Holmes, the most popular novelist of her day, wrote most of her 38 sentimental tales in a busy half century.

Mrs. Holmes placed the scenes of most of her fiction in the South or in her native New England, seldom in the Western New York she knew so well. But in "Cousin Maude" the heroine is a young girl who leaves her New England home, to be met at the end of her long journey at the Canandaigua depot by a farm carriage that takes her over rough roads to "Laurel Hill from whose rocky hillsides she could see the sparkling waters of Honeoye." Perhaps the novelist was harking back to a day in her own girlhood when another New England lass named Mary Jane Hawes came to Allen's Hill to teach school, not far from "the sparkling waters of Honeoye."

Honeoye people insist that the hills around their lake are not the Bristols. They are "the Honeoye hills." The Bristol Hills are to the eastward. And those hills that gird the Bristol Valley have enough beauty and lore of their own without infringing on neighbors.

In 1669, spurred by Indian tales of a magic spring, the Jesuit, Galinee, brought another Frenchman, the famous La Salle, to the Bristol Valley to see the "water that burned." They applied a torch and "the water immediately took fire and burned like brandy." It was the first experience of the white men with a gas fissure.

The Burning Spring still gurgles in a small ravine on the Benjamin Jones farm near Bristol Center. Touch a match to it today and it will burn briefly, just as it did in La Salle's time. Few visit the phenomenon these days. A previous owner, Walter B. Case, had a picnic grounds near the spring and charged admission.

On the same farm farther back in the hills was the Eternal Flame, where a little tongue of fire burned in a dark cave. How it first was lighted no one knows. But during the last few years some shift in the earth, possibly a slight tremor, has extinguished the magic light.

Scattered along the road that threads the Bristol Valley is a procession of hamlets. One of them is Vincent, named for a pioneer physician. Once it was known as Muttonville and between 1830 and 1850 it was America's greatest sheep abattoir. Once there were 50,000 sheep cropping the sparse verdure of the Bristols. They combed it so thoroughly that in some places the land has been sterile ever since.

Those were grim days. The roads were choked with droves of whimpering sheep being led to the slaughter. The fence posts of Asa Gooding's farm and others were covered with drying pelts. Vultures hovered above in low circling formations. The pelts were tanned and made into gloves, shoes and coats. Some of the meat found its way to faraway markets. As many as 1,000 candles a day were made out of the mutton fat.

Changing times and the opening of the West ended Muttonville's reign as the sheep and mutton center. Now Vincent is just another hamlet in the valley.

That valley was the center of another industry not so long ago. For some 70 years the growing of hops was a flourishing business and the hop fields once covered 2,000 acres of Bristol land. Production began in 1835 when seedlings were imported from England. The fields brought fortune to many an owner, disaster to others who tried to "outguess the market."

For three weeks in late August or early September, a mighty army of hop pickers, men, women and children from far and near, invaded the valley. The women pickers not of the neighborhood slept in the farmhouses, the men in the hop houses on straw-filled ticks. The Fall harvest was a gay time and the strains of the dancing fiddles sounded nightly.

Men and women who picked hops in the Bristols long ago may remember seeking "the Kiss-Me-Quick," the flower that in the hop fields has the same sentimental meaning as the red ear at corn-husking time.

Few hops have been grown in this area since 1921. New ingredients for beverages, combined with prohibition, mould and pests, doomed the hop fields. No more do the growers plant the roots in the Spring and set the 25-foot poles, some of which came from Canada, in the ground. Those same poles were pulled out in the Fall. The smell of the sulphur fires in the basements of the drying houses no longer scents the air. The hop fields have joined covered bridges and buffalo robes in limbo.

The wooded peaks in the Bristols are among the highest in Upstate New York. Gannett Hill, where Frank Gannett, the newspaper publisher, was born, is 2,256 feet above seaboard. Some claim Tabor Corners Hill, nine miles south of Honeoye, is four feet higher. But it does not have the dizzy abyss, called the "Jump Off," that yawns just west of the mountain peak that is Gannett Hill.

The Atomic Age has brought many city folks to the picturesque land of the Burning Spring and the "finger lying" lake in the hills. But there are few communities where so many generations have clung to the land on which their forefathers settled. There are still Blackmers and Allens and Reeds in Honeoye village and Garlinghouses on Allen's Hill. And for 120 years, up to 1943, a Gilbert kept store in Honeoye village.

*　　*　　*

Hemlock is a captive lake. Long ago the arm of an industrial city reached out to claim the six miles of narrow water as its own. It chained the hill-girt lake to its chariot wheel with long links of iron pipe hidden under Genesee Valley earth.

Through the years Hemlock and her fellow captive, her radiant smaller sister, Canadice, have served their metropolitan mistress well. Daily they mix a 38 million gallon cocktail for the big city to the northward. Yet the thirst of the city seems as boundless as has been the pride of Rochester for more than 75 years in her pure upland water supply.

But Hemlock is no mere drab faithful old retainer. She is a wild and elfin child of the forest. None of the lakes of the Genesee Country has more physical allure. The northward-bound traveler, climbing upward from the lush Springwater Valley on the wide straight road that leads from the Southern Tier to Rochester, catches his first glimpse of Hemlock's slender grace. Sometimes the trees on the steep banks momentarily hide her from view. She is the more enchanting for her elusiveness.

Hemlock is a mountain lake although the innate conservatism of her people will never let them call old Bald Hill or her other rugged guardians anything but plain "hills."

In the Indian tongue, Hemlock is Onehda and she is as rich in history and legend as she is in physical charm and utility.

In distant days before the Senecas became masters of this domain, tribal fires, probably Algonkian, glowed on her wooded hills. The lake was a favorite hunting ground for the Indians and the braves came to her Eagle Rock to hear the echo of their own voices and in their simple faith to believe they were communing with departed tribesmen.

Then in 1779 over an old Indian trail, made almost impassable by rains, General Sullivan's army marched over the hills from Honeoye, dragging its artillery through the narrow defiles. After destroying fields of Indian corn on the flats, the Yankee soldiers forded the lake at its shallow foot and crossed the Marrowback range to bivouac at Conesus Lake.

In 1790 the first white pioneers came. Mostly they were New Englanders, skillful with the ax and, if needs be, with gun or fist. The whine of saws echoed over the waters and the place, first called Slab City, because so many houses of wooden slabs were built there, arose. That lumber town later was renamed Hemlock.

The pioneers were forthright men. Sometimes they took the law in their own hands. For instance there was "the dam war" of 1825. After the completion of the Erie Canal dams were built at Western New York lakes as feeders for the Clinton Ditch. It turned out the canal did not need them but the dammed-up water was very convenient for the owners of saw mills at the Hemlock outlet. In Spring and Fall, the water would back up into the swampy woods at the head of the lake. In the summer it dried up, leaving decaying substances that caused fevers.

The settlers at the head of the lake tired of that condition and demanded that the dam be removed. The mill owners were deaf to their demands. One summer's day 200 farmers mobilized and came down to the foot of the lake, with axes, crowbars and ropes. They proceded to dismantle the dam and gates. The Slab City mill owners protested—and then begged. The farmers yielded, the work of destruction halted and the "army" disbanded. But the next year the settlers got permission from the state to remove the rest of the dam.

In 1866 a horde of squatters settled on the Springwater flats. After the land owners ousted them, a riotous time ensued, with barns burned and cattle slaughtered. Finally the two forces met in pitched battle. The landowners won and the squatters departed for good.

Hemlock Lake had its day—and a pleasant one it was—as a summer resort. Once there were 100 cottages and five hotels along her shores and five steamboats on her waters.

Those were the days of the Half Way House, the Port House, at the head of Hemlock; the Lake Shore Hotel and dance hall; the St. James from which all lake tours started, and the three-story Jacques, at the northwestern edge, with its spacious piazzas.

The first steamboat on the lake was the Seth Green, launched in 1874 to the strains of the Lima Cornet Band. Then came the Mollie Tefft, owned by a Rochester woman of that name; H. J. Wemett's Cora Belle; the Nellie, later renamed the A. Bronson, and the Wave.

That era ended when Rochester's need for Hemlock water became more insistent and eventually the city not only took over the lake but most of the land along its shores. Still the steamboat-cottage days lingered for a time after the city tapped the upland water.

In 1872 Rochester decided to build its own water system and turned to Hemlock because of the purity of its water which could be sent coursing down the hills by gravity flow.

The first conduit was begun in 1873 and the water first ran through the pipes on Jan. 22, 1876. In 1877 thirty miles of pole line was constructed between Rochester and Hemlock Lake. It was then the longest telephone line in the world. As Mr. Bell's invention was new and unproved, the line was equipped with Morse instruments, as well as telephones—just in case.

The building of conduit No. 2 in 1893-94 brought a considerable boom to the region. About that time the city began buying up large acreages around the lake and the cottages, hotels and boats began to disappear. The third conduit was built in 1914-18. Recently new conduits have been installed and the storage facilities of the lakes are being increased.

Hemlock Village, a bit of transplanted New England, sprawls for more than a mile along the main street. For 81 years, except for a brief intermission during World War 2, Hemlock has been the scene of "The Slab City World's Fair," an institution in the upland country. It's a genuine old fashioned country fair and draws crowds from Livonia, Honeoye, Canadice Corners, Allen's Hill and Taber's Corners, and the whole countryside as well as from Rochester. In its banner year 22,000 passed through the turnstiles of the "World's Fair."

In the Fall of 1949 the name of Hemlock splashed into the national headlines. Eleven-year-old Joanne Lynn left her home south of the village on a September morning to walk down a well-traveled highway to the Hemlock School. She was never seen alive again. No one saw the car that must have picked her up. After six days of searching by state troopers, sheriff's men, citizens and National Guardsmen, a girl looking for chestnuts in a field south of Lima came upon the Lynn girl's body. She had been the victim of a pervert slayer. The crime aroused the whole countryside but as this is written, the murderer is still at large.

On a hill above the west shore of Hemlock Lake, a square, four-story stone building stands out in bold relief against the green woods. It is St. Michael's Mission House, where dwell and labor members of the order known as the Brothers of the Divine Word. The order was founded in Holland and has few branches in the Eastern United States. At St. Michael's students receive preparatory training for mission fields. On the grounds of the mission house, the good brothers have carved out of the rocky soil two grottoes that house statues of the saints. The dim light in the caves, the sacred shrines give a medieval air to the mission above Hemlock water.

The site was once the country home of the Most Rev. Bernard J. McQuaid, first Catholic Bishop of Rochester. There he planted a vineyard on the slopes above the lake to provide sacramental wine for the diocese. The Brothers of the Divine Word have expanded that vineyard until today they have a flourishing commercial wine business, besides supplying churchly needs.

*　　*　　*

"*A beautiful lake is the Canadice,*
　　And wild fowl dream on its broad expanse;
　　The golden brooch of costly price
　　Is dim with its radiant wave compared."

So wrote the bard of Avon N. Y., W. C. H. Hosmer, long ago.

Over in Ontario County, east of Hemlock, lies its radiant sister, Canadice, sparkling among wooded hills.

Canadice is only four miles long, but its Indian name means "long lake." For more than half a century it has, like Hemlock, been a captive of the city. It has given generously of its cool, spring-fed water as an auxiliary arm of Rochester's supply. Once Canadice had many cottages and was a picnic spot. In those days Pete Moose's place on the east shore was a popular rendezvous. Now Canadice's day as a resort is memory. Every private residence on the lake has gone. It belongs to Rochester's water system but its natural beauty is undimmed.

> "A beautiful lake is the Canadice,
> And tribesmen dwelt on its banks of yore,
> But a hundred years have vanished thrice,
> Since hearthstones smoked upon its shores."

An ancient legend clings to the little lake in the woods. In the 15th Century, a peaceful Indian people dwelt on a hill above Canadice's western shore. A fierce and warlike tribe raided their settlement and killed every human there save Onnolee, the beautiful wife of a chief. The fair prisoner was tied to the red belt of the savage chief of the invaders and was dragged away from her ravaged home. When the chief relaxed his vigilance for a moment, Onnolee, quick as light, seized the hunting knife from her captor's belt and plunged it into his side. Then knowing her life was forfeit and while arrows sang past her head, she ran to the lake and chanting the death song of her people, "from the high rocks sprang."

And they say that in the time of falling leaves, when the moonlight shines on Canadice, a graceful, shadowy form is seen to rise from the bosom of the gem-like lake and a plaintive song is heard in a strange tongue.

*　　*　　*

The theme song of the "little Finger Lake" that lies nearest to Rochester's southern door is "In the Good Old Summertime." For generations Conesus Lake has been a Summer playground for Rochester and the Genesee Valley.

Its 18 miles of leafy shore, from Lakeville at its foot to the Cedar Swamp at its head, are lined with summer cottages. Some are pretentious stucco residences, like those at Eagle Point which got its name long ago from the lordly birds that nested there. There also are three-room cabins that humble men built with hard-earned dollars that they too might be masters of a "Rest-a-While" or a "Bide-a-Wee" on Conesus.

Come Memorial Day and the whole lakeside is astir with rollicking voices. The cottagers have come. Motorboats skim the waters, dodging the boats of the patient fishermen. By night the clatter of the roller skates at McPherson's Point echoes across the narrow water to join the music at Long Point where cottagers and rural folk mingle, as did their fathers and mothers in another day.

Come Labor Day and there is the banging of hammers closing up cottage windows and then the farewells that always include a "See you next Summer." In the twilight the roads are choked with homeward-bound automobiles.

Since before the turn of the century, it has been like that. Only in horse and buggy days the steamboats took the cottagers and their belongings down to Lakeville where the Erie train was waiting at the water's edge.

Gone are the steamboats and the trains. The honk of the "horseless carriage" on paved roads sounded their knell more than three decades ago.

No more does a 20-coach excursion train roll in from Rochester on Summer Sundays. Some Sundays two such trains left the now departed Erie Station in Court Street for Conesus. The 50-cent round trip fare included a "boat ride around picturesque Conesus Lake."

In the late 1890s and early years of this century the Erie ran a daily commuter train from Rochester to Lakeville. Steamboats met the trains and took the commuters to the dock nearest their cottages. In the morning the boat and train would bring dad back to the city and its daily tasks, while mom and the girls would stay at the cottage on the lake.

Among the excursion boats that once plied Conesus waters was the big three-decker McPherson, later renamed the Star Rucca, which could carry more than 1,000 passengers and had a six-man crew. It burned one night at the Lakeville pier after 15 years of service.

The first steamboat on the lake was the Jessie. Then came Dan Walkley's Alice M., which was converted into a gasoline launch and wound up its days at Silver Lake. The steamer H. D. Jaeger was named after the Erie's general passenger agent. Oldtimers will tell you also of the Cyclone, a speed launch that burned; of the Rochester, another gasoline burner; of the J. A. Ritz, whose bow became part of a pig pen on a hillside farm above the lake it once rode so proudly; of Bill Carnes' ferry, the G. A. Thompson, and the two-decker flat-bottomed excursion boat, the Conesus, owned by Walter Strowger.

There are memories of lakeside hotels, some of them gone from the scene. Jerry Bolles' once popular Lake Crest, is now a part of the main building of Stella Maris, the Catholic boys' camp. The big four-story Livingston Inn at McPherson's Point once was the Avon Cure, a sanitarium during the heyday of Avon Springs as a health resort. It was torn down and moved in sections by freight gondola and steamboat to the Point where it was reassembled. The Excelsior Springs Hotel, on the far east side of the lake, was built as a water cure because of the mineral springs nearby.

Lakeville is the only community on Conesus shores. It's a busy place in Summer but the docks have gone and the Erie tracks no longer run down to the water's edge. The Winter ice harvest and the huge ice house are memories now. Tragic fire recently visited the old inn that went back to stage coach times. But Acker's general store is still there and Carroll Acker serves the trade as did his father, Frank, before him. The business has been in the family for nearly 90 years.

Once Lakeville was a thriving village in its own right and not so dependent on the Summer trade. In 1821 when Livingston County was formed, it was a formidable rival of haughty Geneseo for the county seat.

Southeast of Lakeville on a commanding hill stands Livonia, named after a Russian province and settled by New Englanders, a trading center for a large area and often swept by fire in recent years. The first settler in the town came in 1789 from Litchfield, Conn., alone on foot, with his gun, ax and pack on his back. His name was Solomon Woodruff. He built a log house and went back East for his wife. On their return they found the Indians had burned the cabin.

In a primitive time the Red Men built a mound-like fortification near the outlet of the lake that they called Gahn-yuh-sas, from the sheep berries that grew on its shores. In the 18th Century, a Seneca village of log houses stood among orchards and fields of corn at the head of the lake.

General Sullivan's expedition marched over the hills from Hemlock Lake and came upon this village. All its inhabitants had fled, leaving a rich crop of corn standing in the fields.

The Yankees destroyed the village and the crops and encamped nearby for the night. It was from this base that a scouting party of 26 men under young Lieutenant Thomas Boyd went out to reconnoiter the principal Seneca village of the Genesee, Chief Little Beard's town, called Genesee Castle, near the present site of Cuylerville.

Boyd's party was observed by two Indians, one of whom fell under the deadly repeating gun of a fabulous scout named Timothy Murphy. The other Seneca escaped and spread the alarm. Hastily the scouting party retraced its steps toward the camp. Only a mile from Sullivan's base at the head of Conesus Lake, the Senecas under the Mohawk, Joseph Brant, and their Tory allies, led by the ruthless

Walter Butler, lay in ambush in a wooded ravine. There was a sharp, short struggle. The Yankees were hopelessly outnumbered. Fifteen fell on the spot. Boyd and Sergeant Michael Parker were captured and dragged off to Genesee Castle. There they were tortured to death, after they refused to divulge Sullivan's campaign plans.

Out in a field on a hillock overlooking the ravine of the ambuscade, a mile from the west shore of the lake and a short distance from Gray's Corners, stands a plain white shaft, surrounded by an iron fence. It was erected by the Livingston County Historical Society to mark the spot of one of the few engagements ever fought on Genesee Country soil. One who stands today on that hill, in the most peaceful countryside imaginable, finds it hard to believe that once it resounded to savage war whoops, the whizz of arrows, the rattle of musketry and the screams of dying men.

When Sullivan's men took up the march again, they had to build a bridge across the swamp at the head of the lake. A legend still persists that they discarded a three-pound brass cannon in the marsh there. And every few years parties go out in the Cedar Swamp looking for Sullivan's discarded cannon.

Under two tall cedars in the old Union Cemetery near Scottsburg, south of the lake, is a shiny granite marker, bearing this inscription:

CAPT. DANIEL SHAYS, 1747–1825

Shays' Rebellion is in all the history books. In the wake of the Revolution, as so often happens after a war, came a financial depression. It fell heavily on Western Massachusetts, where settlers, many of them veterans of the Revolution, lost their homes, were thrown into jail for debt and generally were having a hard time of it, because of the depreciated national currency and the chaotic times.

Those Bay Staters organized in armed revolt against the "Boston bankers" who held most of the war bonds. Their leader was Daniel Shays, a Revolutionary captain with a gallant record. In 1786 Shays appeared in Springfield at the head of 1,600 men and prevented the Supreme Court of Massachusetts from sitting. The next year he led his rebels again to Springfield and tried to seize the Arsenal. This time the militia was ready. They fired on the mob, which dispersed in disorder. Shays fled to Vermont and his rebellion was over. He was a fugitive with a price upon his head but soon received a pardon.

He left New England and after a brief sojourn near Cayuga Lake, came to the Conesus region in 1817. He was 67 then. With his war pension he bought a farm and built a log house. Then he married a young widow of some means. Pioneers remembered him as a short, stout, rather garrulous old fellow with a fondness for the bottle. He died at the age of 78 and was buried in the old Union Cemetery in his uniform of buff and blue.

In 1814 a boy of 14, large for his age, with long fair hair and a bland, disarming smile that was to stand him in good stead, came from Skaneateles way, on foot to work as an apprentice in a cloth dressing establishment near Scottsburg. His employer put him to work chopping wood and at other menial tasks. The boy rebelled and demanded that he be given a chance to learn the trade. Under threat of bodily harm, the employer yielded and there was no more hewing of wood for the apprentice lad.

His name was Millard Fillmore and he became the thirteenth President of the United States.

Latter day Conesus Lake residents are more interested in such famous residents as Billy Sandow at whose camp the wrestling champ, Ed (Strangler) Lewis once trained and Vic Raschi, the Yankee pitcher, who spends his off-season months at his Conesus home.

Should a superstitious 18th Century Seneca return to his old hunting grounds on the eve of the Fourth of July, he would be startled to see his old lake "on fire." Every year on the eve of the holiday after darkness falls, red flares are lighted in front of every cottage and Conesus is ringed with fire. It's a spectacle worth seeing.

Around this upland lake with the old Indian name will ever linger memories of happy Summers beside the quiet waters—and the hoarse whistles of steamboats whose paddles have long been stilled and the rumble of ghostly excursion trains.